EMDR
for
Depression

**OVERCOME
THE TRAUMA
THAT DRIVES
YOUR
SYMPTOMS**

LARA BARBIR, PsyD

New Harbinger Publications, Inc.

Publisher's Note

NEW HARBINGER PUBLICATIONS is a registered trademark of New Harbinger Publications, Inc.

New Harbinger Publications is an employee-owned company.

Copyright © 2026 by Lara Barbir
New Harbinger Publications, Inc.
5720 Shattuck Avenue
Oakland, CA 94609
www.newharbinger.com

NCEO
MEMBER

Cover design by Amy Shoup

Acquired by Wendy Millstine

Edited by Max Crosby

Library of Congress Cataloging-in-Publication Data on file

FSC
www.fsc.org
MIX
Paper | Supporting
responsible forestry
FSC® C008955

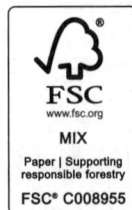

Printed in the United States of America

28   27   26

10   9   8   7   6   5   4   3   2   1   First Printing

For all of the yous—past, present, and future…

Contents

CHAPTER 1

The Problem: It's Probably Depression and Trauma

What you resist not only persists, but will grow in size.

—Carl Jung

People are used to seeing the side of you that's strong, positive, and functioning well, but internally, you feel lost, alone, and confused. It might feel like you're failing at life. You have become more detached, disconnected, and numb, with the exception of bouts of intense anxiety or anger—neither of which are typical for the real you. If you've been curious and courageous enough to break through some of these psychological walls, you may have found a dark part of yourself beneath them that feels inherently flawed, worthless, and insignificant. While down there in this discouraging abyss, you may have noticed starting to question whether you ever felt connected, finding yourself filled with doubts about everything and everyone that surrounds you, especially yourself.

But then you start to feel more out of control, which then starts to manifest in certain behaviors you've adopted to cope with these painful experiences—like pouring your energy into work in unfulfilling ways, engaging in addictive or obsessive-compulsive behaviors, isolating yourself, or withdrawing from or otherwise avoiding your once-typical engagements. You may not know how much longer you can keep up this façade you've been wearing, so you might be trying to eliminate these habits. On one hand, this can feel empowering, but on the other, you might start feeling worse because you no longer have those ways of coping or distracting yourself.

Maybe you've had episodes like this in the past in similar contexts, but not to the degree where you've actually wanted to do something about it. Take a few moments in silence with yourself to consider when you noticed that you started struggling most recently. Notice what thoughts, feelings, memories, situations, or people come to the surface. What are the major stressors in your life right now? Chances are that you noticed your personal struggles becoming more active in the midst of a relationship, school, health, work, or other personal conflict or change.

Take another few moments to consider this: when do you remember first noticing you were struggling in life? Whatever age comes to mind is relevant. Take note of what conflicts or changes were occurring. Looking at more recent stressors compared to that time, do you notice any patterns that seem significant?

What Is Depression?

If any of the above experiences have resonated with you, the problem is certainly both complex and unique to your personal history. However, to summarize it simply, it can probably be best captured by the term depression. Know that you are not alone as you are about to learn more about how common and underestimated depression actually is. Hopefully the statistics shared below can help you in your recovery by demonstrating that depression is a universal problem rather than a personal flaw or defect.

- According to the World Health Organization (2023b), 280 million people around the globe suffer from depression, and it is one of the leading causes of disability worldwide. Depression is the most common mental disorder in the US and the strongest risk factor for suicidal behavior.

- A 2020 survey found that 9.2% of Americans aged 12 years and older experienced a past-year major depressive episode, with young adults aged 18-25 years (17.2%) and adolescents aged 12-17 years (16.9%) being most commonly impacted (Goodwin et al. 2022).

- These numbers unfortunately largely underrepresent the true prevalence of depression; research suggests an estimated 35-50% of people with depression go unrecognized each year (Magnus, Shankar, & Broussard 2010). This might be due to a combination of reasons, such as the lack of access to healthcare, the stigma around seeking both personal and professional help, and the ability of the brain to deny or repress symptoms.

- The World Health Organization (2022) stated that since the onset of the coronavirus pandemic in 2019, the prevalence of depression increased by 25% globally and disproportionately affected younger people and women; importantly, this increase has remained even after the restrictions on quarantining and isolating were lifted.

- In the US, a 2023 Gallup panel survey revealed that 29% of adults reported having been diagnosed with depression at some point in their lifetime, which is nearly 20 percentage points higher than recorded in 2015. The poll also showed that 17.8% of Americans currently have or are being treated for depression, which is over 10 percentage points higher than in 2015. According to Gallup, these rates are the highest ever recorded.

- Equally astoundingly, rates of lifetime incidence of depression have increased from 26.2% in 2017 to 36.7% in 2023 among women, and from 17.7% in 2017 to 20.4% in 2023 for men.

It's important to know how depression has been defined in the health care field. Health care professionals use the term *major depressive disorder* to describe a range of symptoms someone may experience for more days than not over at least a two-week period. These symptoms range in both presentation and severity—from "mild" to "severe"—and typically affect a person's mood, energy, attitude, thoughts, feelings, and behaviors. A person can experience a single episode or have recurrent episodes over time that last for at least two weeks; the latter is often referred to as recurrent or chronic depression. A person can also experience these symptoms persistently in a mild manner, which is known as *dysthymia*. As you can imagine, these symptoms can disrupt one's ability to function as usual across different life domains, such as work, school, sleep, leisure, and relationships, causing significant distress. Common symptoms of depression include the following:

- Persistently feeling down, depressed, or hopeless; or a low level of persistent irritability (a more common presentation for men)

- Little interest or pleasure in doing things that were once enjoyed

- Trouble falling or staying asleep or, alternatively, sleeping too much

- Appetite changes, which sometimes lead to noticeable weight loss or gain

- Increased feelings of fatigue or low energy

- Excessive feelings of guilt, shame, inadequacy, or worthlessness

- Trouble concentrating—more than what's considered typical

- Feeling either more agitated and restless or more slowed in movement and speech

- Thoughts of hurting or killing oneself or thinking that one would be better off dead

Simply having a few of these symptoms does not automatically mean that a person has depression. It is always important to regularly visit a primary care practitioner to rule out any sort of organic problems, including certain kinds of medications, that could be contributing to having some of these symptoms.

Notice in the symptoms that *excessive* feelings of guilt or shame are listed. Guilt is an emotion that is warranted in situations when our behavior violates our moral code of being and therefore motivates us into the necessary problem-solving to correct any wrongs we committed and prevent them from reoccurring in the future. It's normal to make mistakes—for instance, most of us might make the mistake of losing our cool with a loved one when under stress. Acknowledging that feeling of guilt can motivate us to communicate a heartfelt apology. We may also analyze what went wrong to best ascertain how we can do better in the future. Guilt becomes excessive or unhealthy when there's frequent rumination, or replaying of past events in a self-punishing way, despite making behavioral changes. That is likely when shame is also at play.

Guilt is feeling bad about committing a wrong action ("I *did* something wrong or bad"), whereas shame is more about believing oneself to be inherently flawed, defective, or worthless ("I *am* wrong or bad"). Shame is a primitive emotion that exists for evolutionary reasons: we are more likely to survive in tribes, especially if we are vulnerable or younger. In needing to feel acceptance from and a sense of belonging to our tribe, shame serves to motivate us into hiding whatever it is we feel bad about to avoid being rejected. In this way, shame is connected to our need to feel safe, and so especially at a young age we tend to choose a sense of belonging over a sense of self. If shame is excessive and deeply internalized, however, it can lead someone to withdraw and hide their true selves from others, which can then put them at greater risk for depression.

One commonly used questionnaire you can easily access online to assess symptoms of depression is called the Beck Depression Inventory-II (BDI-II), which can help you begin to better understand some of the ways in which your own depression may manifest as well as how the symptoms may vary for others. You can take the assessment for yourself online—doing so will help you understand your own depression.

However, it's important to remember that assessments can be limiting in the overall view of your experiences with depression. For instance, if you are self-medicating your pain through the use of alcohol, food, drugs, sex or pornography, or other addictive or compulsive behaviors— or you are otherwise repressing or denying your pain, as many of us do to varying degrees—this can lead to an appearance of lesser severity or even false negatives on screening questionnaires. Take a moment to also consider that, as part of a sneaky form of denial, pain tied to depression can manifest as physical ailments when not appropriately addressed, including but not limited to chronic muscle or joint pain, inflammation, autoimmune diseases, gastrointestinal problems, headaches, and migraines.

Take a moment to pause and reflect on the reactions your mind and body are having to these statistics and to the assessment. You might journal about your emotions, process the results with a loved one or therapist, or a combination of the above. Knowing that you're not alone in your experience of depression is both important and validating. Nevertheless, it's also equally important and validating for your recovery to notice, acknowledge, and share what's happening for you in this moment.

Depression Treatments

Given the substantial increase and persistence in reports of depression worldwide, properly detecting and treating depression have never been more important. Although psychotherapeutic interventions have been long established for the treatment of depression, the barriers are multifold. For one, treatment can be difficult to access. The World Health Organization (2023a) pointed out that as of 2021, 4.5 billion people—more than half of the world's population—do not have sufficient access to healthcare, and another 2 billion people go into severe financial hardship when finding care. Moreover, even when treatment is accessible, it is not always successful in the long-term—particularly for those with recurrent or chronic depression. For instance, one study found that 29% of those who responded to acute-phase cognitive-behavioral therapies relapsed after one year, and 54% relapsed after two years (Vittengl et al. 2007).

The unfortunate likelihood of "relapse" into depression after treatment, while likely explained by a number of various factors, suggests in part that we are not treating it sufficiently. One hypothesis to explain why this may be occurring is that we do not fully understand it—as in the treatment being used is not quite getting to the very root of the depression.

Depression is complex. It can manifest in myriad ways and is unique to each person experiencing it. It is not always obvious on the surface, even for a trained mental health professional, because of the possibility of a person hiding it well. Likewise, it is typically influenced by multiple factors—some of which are not controllable—across biological, social, psychological, cultural, and spiritual domains, and the interaction among these. Nevertheless, from a psychological treatment standpoint there is room for improvement in more fully comprehending true roots of depression.

Understanding Trauma and Its Impact on Depression

Researchers have suggested that placing greater emphasis on the influence of traumatic experiences and adverse life events on depression's development and progression is important in order to further improve treatment effects and lower relapse rates (Hase et al. 2018, Yehuda et al. 2012). Why consider trauma? Depression may be the most common condition following trauma (Adshead & Ferris 2007), and it is the most common comorbid diagnosis with post-traumatic stress disorder (PTSD), concurrent up to 56%, and with a lifetime co-occurrence of 95% (Bleich et al. 1997, Shalev et al. 1998).

Individuals may be diagnosed with depression without co-occurring PTSD despite having experienced trauma, simply because their symptom presentation did not meet the full criteria for a PTSD diagnosis. There is much overlap between depression and trauma when looking at the impact on thoughts, feelings, and behaviors as depicted in the figure below. For instance, depression and trauma typically have not-always-fully-conscious commonalities in the form of disrupted core beliefs about self and others, unaddressed ruptures in early attachments to caregivers, and immense feelings of guilt, shame, helplessness, sadness, loss, and grief. Similarly, the symptoms that affect both depression and trauma can narrow one's *window of tolerance* for experiencing distress, making one hypersensitive to becoming emotionally dysregulated to such an extreme that the rational brain, which is necessary for processing information, is turned off. This can manifest into one of two extremes: becoming either easily shut down, numb, or disconnected from emotions (also called "hypoaroused"), or easily startled and sent into a panic state (also called "hyperaroused").

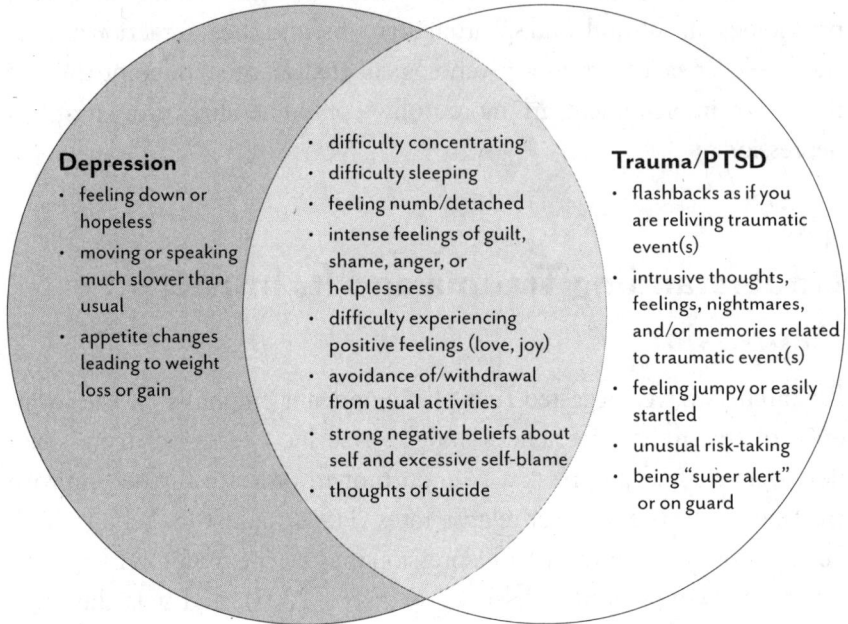

Depression
- feeling down or hopeless
- moving or speaking much slower than usual
- appetite changes leading to weight loss or gain

- difficulty concentrating
- difficulty sleeping
- feeling numb/detached
- intense feelings of guilt, shame, anger, or helplessness
- difficulty experiencing positive feelings (love, joy)
- avoidance of/withdrawal from usual activities
- strong negative beliefs about self and excessive self-blame
- thoughts of suicide

Trauma/PTSD
- flashbacks as if you are reliving traumatic event(s)
- intrusive thoughts, feelings, nightmares, and/or memories related to traumatic event(s)
- feeling jumpy or easily startled
- unusual risk-taking
- being "super alert" or on guard

Despite the fact that it has been well-established that childhood trauma plays a significant role in the development, recurrence, and severity of depression, addressing trauma is not often a primary focus in gold standard psychological treatments for depression (Chapman et al. 2004, Edwards et al. 2003, Felitti et al. 1998, Kendler et al. 1993, Kendler et al. 2000, Nelson et al. 2002, Waite & Shewokis 2012). Childhood trauma not only includes maltreatment due to acts of commission or acts of omission but also parental loss due to death or separation (Agid et al. 1999). The most important research study that established the impact of childhood trauma on the development of adult depression is called the Adverse Childhood Experiences, or ACE study—a decade-long longitudinal study of 17,000 predominantly white middle-class American adults conducted during the mid-1990s. The following definitions of childhood trauma as defined by this study are provided to help you better understand the many kinds of maltreatment captured by this umbrella term:

Abuse

- **Emotional abuse**: A caregiver or adult living in your home often put you down through extremely negative criticisms, insults, or humiliation, or acted in a way that made you afraid for your physical safety.

- **Physical abuse**: A caregiver or adult living in your home pushed, grabbed, slapped, or threw something at you, or physically hurt you in such a way that you had visible marks or were injured.

- **Sexual abuse**: An adult, relative, family friend, or stranger who was at least five years older than you touched or fondled your body in a sexual way, made you touch their body in a sexual way, or attempted to have any type of sexual relationship with you.

Neglect

- **Emotional neglect**: Someone in your family never or rarely helped you feel important or special, you never or rarely felt loved, people in your family never or rarely looked out for each other and felt close to each other, or your family was never or rarely a source of strength and support.

- **Physical neglect**: There was never or rarely a caregiver present to help take care of you, protect you, or take you to get medical attention when you needed it; your basic needs for food were not consistently met, your caregiver was too drunk or high to take care of you, or you had to wear dirty clothing.

Other Related Household Challenges

- **Parent treated violently**: Your parent or stepparent was physically abused (e.g., pushed, grabbed, slapped, had something thrown at them, kicked, bitten, hit with a fist or something hard, or threatened or hurt by a knife or gun) by your other parent or their significant other.

- **Substance abuse in the household**: A household member had problems with drug or alcohol abuse.

- **Parental separation or divorce**: Your parents were ever separated or divorced.

- **Incarcerated household member**: A household member went to prison.

The ACE questionnaire is included below for you to better understand yourself, first and foremost. Please take note that the questions as well as the statistics shared below the questionnaire may provoke some emotional reactions. It is important that you practice giving yourself a space of acceptance—meaning without judging your experience—to be lovingly present with whatever reactions arise.

While you were growing up, during your first 18 years of life:

1. Did a parent or other adult in the household often…swear at you, insult you, put you down, or humiliate you? Or act in a way that made you afraid that you might be physically hurt? If yes, enter 1 _____

2. Did a parent or other adult in the household often…push, grab, slap, or throw something at you? Or ever hit you so hard that you had marks or were injured? If yes, enter 1 _____

3. Did an adult or person at least five years older than you ever…touch or fondle you or have you touch their body in a sexual way? Or try to or actually have oral, anal, or vaginal sex with you? If yes, enter 1 _____

4. Did you often feel that…no one in your family loved you or thought you were important or special? Or your family didn't look out for each other, feel close to each other, or support each other? If yes, enter 1 _____

5. Did you often feel that…you didn't have enough to eat, had to wear dirty clothes, and had no one to protect you? Or your parents were too drunk or high to take care of you or take you to the doctor if you needed it? If yes, enter 1 _____

6. Were your parents ever separated or divorced? If yes, enter 1 _____

7. Was your mother or stepmother… often pushed, grabbed, slapped, or had something thrown at her? Or sometimes or often kicked, bitten, hit with a fist, or hit with something hard? Or ever repeatedly hit over at least a few minutes or threatened with a gun or a knife? If yes, enter 1 _____

8. Did you live with anyone who was a problem drinker or alcoholic or who used street drugs? If yes, enter 1 _____

9. Was a household member depressed or mentally ill or did a household member attempt suicide? If yes, enter 1 _____

10. Did a household member go to prison? If yes, enter 1 _____

Now add up your "Yes" answers: This is your ACE Score. Scores that are greater than 3 are considered to be significant; the higher the score, the greater the impact of life experiences. Learn more at http://www.cdc.gov/violenceprevention/aces/index.html.

As you may have already deduced, this landmark study found a strong relationship between the number of ACEs and general mental health problems in adulthood. This means the greater the number of adverse childhood experiences study participants reported, the greater the number and severity of mental health problems they reported experiencing in adulthood, including the presence of a depressive episode in the past year or lifetime chronic depression. Astoundingly, there was a *four-fold* increase in the risk of depression in people with multiple ACEs, which implies your chances of having depression as an adult are four times more likely if you've experienced multiple childhood traumas. The implications of these findings were further strengthened in a subsequent study of chronically depressed patients in which researchers found that 75.6% of the patients reported childhood trauma, with 37% of these patients reporting multiple childhood traumatization (Negele et al. 2015). In summary, if we are really trying to understand and heal the roots of depression, we should be focusing more on making the connection to and healing the impact from childhood trauma.

To demonstrate that these results apply across more diverse populations and to further examine the links between specific types of childhood trauma and adult depression, the findings of the ACE study were replicated in a subsequent study examining the relationships between ACEs and depression among low-income ethnic minority adult populations residing in an urban setting (Waite & Shewokis 2012). The researchers from this study also concluded that individuals who experienced the following ACEs have greater risk for adult depression:

- Emotional, physical, and/or sexual abuse;

- Emotional neglect;

- Mother treated violently; and

- Living with someone who was depressed, mentally ill, or attempted suicide.

To build upon and refine these researchers' conclusions, the last important piece of research to share with you is from what is called a meta-analysis. These types of analyses are particularly powerful because they compile nearly all of the studies that have already been conducted on a specific topic to then analyze the results, which can reveal significant patterns and provide more robust conclusions. This relevant meta-analysis investigated exposure to various types of childhood trauma in adult participants to have a clearer sense of the relationships between each type of early trauma and depression. The researchers found that of the types of childhood trauma assessed, *emotional abuse* and *neglect* were associated with the highest risk for experiencing depressive disorders in adulthood compared to other kinds of childhood trauma, followed by sexual abuse, domestic violence, and physical abuse (Mandelli et al. 2015). To help you identify what emotional abuse and neglect might entail, the following is a list of common forms:

- Frequent negative criticisms, whether through questioning your decisions, performance, or appearance

- Name-calling in ways that are insulting, demeaning, punishing, or humiliating; this can be done privately or publicly in front of others

- Threats and intimidation to hurt, humiliate, or abandon you

- Invalidating, mocking, or trivializing your feelings

- Passive-aggressive behaviors such as giving silent treatment or withholding affection rather than communicating feelings and resolving problems directly

If you haven't done so already, take a moment to think about these results and observe your reactions. Based on your own experiences, consider whether or not they resonate with you. Even if you have not already begun doing inner work with your own self-education or therapy experience, chances are that you noticed some emotional reactions or physical sensations in your body while reading some of these conclusions—this is totally normal and to be expected.

Use any reactions you observe as opportunities to practice being gentle with yourself. You might need a walk, a meditation, or a talk with or hug from a loved one who supports you well. Engaging in something comforting might be beneficial before you continue reading, though the exercise below is intended to help you access such comforting and nurturing feelings when you need them. We'll talk more about acceptance and self-compassion in later chapters.

Attachment Figure Resource Exercise

When you were upset as a young child, which adult could you turn to who could reliably and consistently help you feel better about yourself? If someone clear comes to mind—a trusted parent, grandparent, other relative, neighbor, teacher, coach, or mentor—trust that! Picture them as the caring and protective figure that they were (and possibly still are) for you, and notice how you feel in your body as you imagine them comforting you with a warm embrace. Give yourself permission to be fully present with the comforting feelings associated with their support in your mind's eye.

If you did not have an adult figure who was *consistently* and *reliably* available to protect and nurture you, you are like many who picked up this book. Know that you are not alone, you are loved, and you belong. Appreciate both what you can draw from your memory of nurturing or protective adults at various points in your life, plus the power of your imagination as you consider the following:

- Who would have been nice to have in the neighborhood who you could have visited as a child? This could be a grandparent-like figure, an aunt or uncle-like figure, a teacher-like figure, or a parent-like figure who lives near you and is consistently available to you. This person might be imaginary, although they also might borrow qualities from people who have been in your life who treated you like you were special and important (but perhaps they were not readily available to you). Trust whoever instinctively shows up in your mind as it is speaking to what you were and are needing for comfort.

- Can you imagine the size of this person and how a hug from them might feel to you now?

- How would you imagine this person showing that they cared for you? Again, trust whatever comes to mind in how you are being comforted. Perhaps you're considering how they nurture you through their soothing touch, words, food, or play. Give yourself permission to be fully present with any comforting and warm feelings associated with their presence in your mind's eye.

- If this person hasn't seen you in a while and you went to see them, how would they greet you? How else might they show you that you're special and important? Again, allow yourself to experience comforting feelings fully. Notice how it feels in your body to simply be present with this person.

- What would this person do if another child in the neighborhood was being mean to you? Notice how it feels in your body to be protected by this person.

- If you were encountering difficulties at school or with friends, how would this person be able to help you figure out these problems? Again, notice and allow yourself to be fully present with how it feels in your body to be helped and guided by this person.

- If during these prompts you noticed feelings of grief coming up tied to the lack of safety, protection, nurturance, and guidance the child in you experienced, try to also make space to be fully present with these feelings as they are completely natural and important to acknowledge. You're already doing an amazing job turning toward your inner experience rather than reinforcing neglecting it. Wounds need your attendance, nurturing, and care in order for them to sufficiently heal.

Note that this exercise and many other helpful worksheets and audio recordings are also available on the free tools site for this book: http://www.newharbinger.com/56975.

Summary

As you've learned, childhood trauma and depression are often seen together. This isn't always the case, especially as we are still learning the root causes of depression, both biological and environmental. It's important to recognize that your symptoms likely developed as a reaction to what you experienced. You are not wrong or bad for having these feelings or issues—you were surviving, and these are common reactions to trauma. Approaching this journey with compassion and empathy will be crucial, as self-criticism usually leads to more negative feelings.

Seeing more of yourself through these assessments is just a starting point, but hopefully you've gained some understanding of what depression is and where it stems from. It might also have given you some insight into the roots of it, looking at your lived experiences to date. Understanding will continue to come slowly the deeper you dive into this work.

Your evolving self-understanding will help you see your experiences with greater compassion, and that compassion will help you reach a space of greater acceptance. Ultimately, acceptance is the proposed method and mechanism for truly overcoming depression. While you cannot go back and change what happened to you, you can embark on the challenging albeit meaningful journey of acceptance. It's important to emphasize that acceptance is more of an internal than an external journey—that is, acceptance of your inner world, *not* of what happened on the outside, is needed.

This book intends to be an essential tool on your journey to healing your depression from its earliest roots using integrative, acceptance-based techniques and a particular type of trauma therapy called Eye Movement Desensitization Reprocessing, or EMDR, to facilitate deeper self-understanding and acceptance. Further information about acceptance and EMDR therapy for depression are covered next in chapter 2. Stay tuned for more on some key ingredients for this journey in chapter 3.

In chapters 4–8, you will learn how to work through the eight phases of EMDR therapy to more deeply uncover and address the roots of depression to facilitate acceptance and gain a more confident, connected, and secure sense of yourself. *It is generally recommended that you work through most of the reprocessing phases with an EMDR therapist,* but there are many EMDR resourcing and other exploratory exercises that you can complete on your own throughout the book. Chapter 9 will provide some steps to consider in integrating your gains as you move forward. The final notes conclude with a summary of what you've learned from embarking on the journey this book guides you through.

Congratulations on the steps you are taking toward a deeper self-love! The investment you're making in yourself is paradoxically some of the most selfless work you can do for human evolution on a large scale. Aside from setting yourself up with an EMDR therapist, other external necessities you'll need to maximize your success include a quiet and safe space, journal, and writing utensil. You can find additional resources and exercises to accompany this book at www.newharbinger.com/56975. As for the internal necessities you'll need, we are going to be covering all of those in depth along the journey, so simply try to adopt an attitude of openness to continued learning while also giving yourself permission to absorb what you learn at a slow and steady pace.

CHAPTER 2

The Solution: Acceptance via EMDR

The curious paradox is that when I accept myself just as I am, then I can change.

—Carl R. Rogers

When we trace depression back to its roots, as we did in chapter 1, we discover that trauma from adverse childhood experiences—particularly the experiences that involved emotional abuse and neglect—is often the seed from which depression sprouts. Looking at it in this frame, we can see that depression is a response to trauma—an attempt to find calm and safety in a place where we desperately needed it. Reminding yourself of this is crucial; remember it's not a reflection of who you are as a person. You were simply doing what it took to survive and adapt to your experiences. Try to gently stop yourself if you notice your mind going down the unhelpful rabbit hole of negative self-criticism or judgments. Instead, focus with a gentle curiosity on exploring the intentions and functions behind the behaviors you've developed to adapt and cope—how have they helped you?

We cannot change the past—there is no way to go back and alter what has already happened to you. Therefore, acceptance is the ideal solution in your journey to healing from and transcending your depression. A key word to remind yourself of in this process is *learning*. Acceptance does not happen overnight; however, you *can* learn to accept, give yourself grace, and keep moving forward with trust and faith. It is a challenging but meaningful journey that tests and strengthens your patience, persistence, courage, and openness—the kinds of traits that will help you live life with more ease, freedom, and trust.

In other words, it's wholeheartedly worth it because you are worth it. Over time, you'll be able to look back with deeper levels of understanding, compassion, and love, all which will better propel you toward creating the life you truly desire. Take a pause to notice any reactions you're having so far. Try to be present to practice just observing them without judgment. "Without judgment" broadly means that whatever you're experiencing in this moment is okay.

What Acceptance Is Not

What exactly does acceptance mean, and how do you know when you have reached a place of acceptance? It may actually help you to first consider what the indications are that you have *not* accepted something. What does it mean to *not accept* something? In service of supporting your sense of self, you're encouraged to first notice, explore, and get curious about your own individual thoughts and answers to this question before reading ahead. Take out a journal or open a Word document and start freely jotting down whatever thoughts and experiences enter your mind. Then practice expressing gratitude that you are giving yourself space to explore your own independent ways of thinking about things. Your self-reflection on your own views about things, especially given your likely history of adverse childhood experiences, deserves attention and appreciation. The more you create that quiet space to connect with your individual experience, the more you will find the answers you're seeking. For instance, you might start or end your journaling entry with an affirmation like, "I'm proud of myself for making space for my thoughts and feelings about this. My inner voice matters."

While your answers to the question of what acceptance is *not* will vary, depending on your experiences, notice how your body reacted when you engaged in answering this question. A big sign you haven't accepted something is that you still physically or emotionally feel something about it—or that you are engaging in those "problematic" behaviors and thought patterns mentioned above and in chapter 1 to cope, whether consciously or not. Deep down below what you see on the surface, you might still be feeling angry, resentful, devastated, sad, anxious, guilty, ashamed, despairing, grief-stricken, or fearful—especially when you are reminded of it. You may also notice dreams recurring that are either directly or indirectly related to it. Indications of nonacceptance might also involve ruminative, intrusive thoughts. Interestingly, the rumination that often occurs in the context of depression is typically a more intellectual or thinking-prone manifestation of some of the feelings mentioned above such as guilt or shame.

Barriers to Acceptance: Defense Mechanisms

You might then deduce that acceptance means that you no longer feel bad about or ruminate on certain events, situations, people, or other reminders of past trauma. While on the one hand this might be true, it is sometimes tricky to conclude with confidence. Why? Acceptance doesn't always mean that you no longer dwell on something, and this is because we are humans with defense mechanisms that allow us to hide our feelings—even from ourselves!

Being wired for survival comes with being equipped to fight off and avoid pain, hence the reason the most basic defense mechanism of *denial* exists. Defenses are useful in that there are times and contexts in which it is not safe or appropriate to be in touch with your emotions and you need to keep your guard up to protect yourself. For instance, *compartmentalization*, or setting aside and blocking your feelings, is often necessary to get work or other tasks done—especially if you are in public, work, school, or interview settings where having a certain game face and detachment from more vulnerable, painful emotions is considered adaptive and culturally normative. Take a moment to consider times and settings like these where you might appropriately have your guard up. Take another moment to practice appreciating the part of you that is appropriately guarded.

As creatures of habit, we have a tendency to repeat patterns of defending against pain—until we decide to start putting in the conscious effort to make a change. Even if having your defenses up is appropriate in certain situations, it is also appropriate and necessary to eventually de-compartmentalize and face emotions—this helps with acceptance and self-care—and you are encouraged to start this practice if you haven't already. Otherwise, the emotional energies will stay in your body and build up, leading to things like depression and its associated behavioral manifestations and physical ailments.

If you have experienced abuse or neglect, you likely have both a greater tendency to bottle up your emotions and, relatedly, more strongly defined defense mechanisms. This is because these were once necessary means of survival that then became further reinforced and ingrained from living in a chronically chaotic or unstable environment. And defense mechanisms are largely unconscious, in case you weren't aware— pun intended—which is why it's important to be patient with the process of acceptance, and especially skeptical about whether you've accepted the pain associated with traumatic experiences that you've hidden from yourself and others for a long time.

Taking out your journal for further self-reflection before reading the next paragraphs, slowly and gently start to self-inquire about what your own defense mechanisms might look like, and from where or whom they may have been learned. You might start this exploration by looking deeper into some recent situations where you noticed yourself having strong emotional reactions and how you may have automatically defended against or "solved" those reactions. Don't expect yourself to know right off the bat since these are unconscious processes that take time and continuous effort to gain insight into. Rest assured that EMDR therapy, ongoing self-reflection via journaling, other self-awareness-building practices like mindfulness, and the guidance in the following paragraphs will help you further identify and uncover these as well.

Also, consider any unhelpful beliefs you may have adopted from society and others about feeling and expressing emotions, remembering that these beliefs initially formed from messages you received both directly through interactions with caregivers and indirectly through caregivers' modeling. These beliefs play a role in shaping those ingrained habits of defending against your emotions. Some examples of commonly held beliefs that people carry about emotions that may get in the way of acceptance include:

- There are good emotions and there are bad emotions.

- Showing emotions is a sign of weakness.

- There are right and wrong ways to feel in every situation.

- Painful emotions are not important and should be ignored.

- My feelings are not important, valid, or acceptable.

- Being emotional means being out of control.

- Being emotionally vulnerable with others is unsafe.

- If others don't approve of my feelings, then I shouldn't feel the way I do.

- Other people are the best judges of how I'm feeling.

Regardless of what exact beliefs you formed as you unconsciously learned about emotions as a child, if you struggle with allowing yourself to feel your emotions—the most important prerequisite to acceptance— you might struggle with *numbness*. This term is also often used interchangeably with its umbrella term, *dissociation*, which refers to a mental process of disconnecting from thoughts, feelings, memories, or a sense of identity. Numbness can be tricky, because at first it might seem as if you are no longer feeling the emotion, leading you to think you've reached acceptance. However, feeling detached or dissociated from your experience in a numbing sort of way usually means that there are feelings buried beneath the surface. Your early learning experiences have taught you to defend strongly against those more vulnerable feelings, and you might not even know they're there because of the nature of our unconscious, as well as the possible lack of proper caregiver attunement you had associated with experiences of emotional neglect or trauma.

So how in the world do you know if your ingrained defense mechanisms are at play? This is a complex question to answer given our evolving nature and the likelihood that you will continue to reach deeper levels of consciousness as you grow through life. However, we will attempt to reach an answer throughout this book as you enhance your self-awareness with ongoing self-reflection, mindfulness, and EMDR therapy exercises. The more you are willing to open and commit yourself to the journey toward acceptance, the more you will learn about yourself and your unconscious processes.

If emotional numbing or dissociation is a defense mechanism you think you may relate to, one indication that this mechanism is at play is that while you notice you don't experience and can block yourself from pain, you also don't experience joy or loving feelings—even if you have people in your life whom you genuinely love and care for. And that in turn makes you feel detached from your experience which then contributes to depression.

Another indication of your defense mechanisms at play that is sometimes more consciously obvious is when you can logically understand when something seems irrational or untrue, but on an emotional level you notice it not *feeling* like it is true. For example, during an episode of depression you might have moments of strongly feeling lonely and ashamed, believing that you're unlovable or unworthy. You might even argue that you have always felt this way deep down, but sometimes it feels more extreme and unbearable which then may lead to your habits of coping, whether through negative self-talk or certain unhealthy behaviors. Take a moment to notice if you're having a physical or emotional reaction *right now* in relating to such beliefs—and any defense mechanisms that might automatically follow these reactions—so that the points covered next can be demonstrated and therefore better understood.

In your more neutral states, you can probably judge from a more logical perspective that beliefs that you are unlovable or unworthy are extreme and simply not true. You might even start to come up with legitimate evidence from your life experiences to prove that such judgments have no validity. Perhaps if you've shared any of these kinds of darker moments with loved ones, they have combated such thoughts with legitimate evidence against them. Engaging in this process is actually a more developed type of defense mechanism called *rationalization* that cognitive behavioral therapists help their clients acquire, assuming they have not already started developing them on their own. You have probably noticed, however, that despite your tried-and-true efforts in rea-soning and justifying why these beliefs aren't true statements, and pos-sibly others' reassurances that they aren't true statements, they still *feel* like they are true.

As such, the rationalizing strategy just doesn't quite work for you emotionally no matter how many times you have repeatedly tried it—although in this defense mechanism's defense, this doesn't mean that it isn't still useful in the service of self-love and compassion to remind your-self of evidence that shows that you are lovable, worthy, and adequate. When there is such a disagreement or divide like this between your logical mind and your emotional brain, it is a clear indication that 1) defense mechanisms are at play, as they typically are given human nature, and 2) there is something deeper being triggered, usually involving some form of trauma across multiple earlier experiences that needs to be dis-covered, acknowledged, processed, understood, and accepted.

Even if you have not engaged in cognitive behavioral therapy (CBT), you have probably noticed rationalizing your emotions as a way of coping with them. Sometimes this is an adaptive process which can provide relief, albeit typically temporarily, whereas other times it can be a sneaky means of avoiding deeper-rooted painful feelings that require more loving attention, investigation, and nurturance—and therefore a way of per-petuating dissociation. In other words, rationalizing your emotions can actually be a devious form of dissociating from them as they arise in the present moment. Other defense mechanisms that similarly involve an over-engagement of the rational, problem-solving brain and a dissocia-tion from the emotional brain include *intellectualization* and *minimiza-tion*, both of which serve to keep you engaging in patterns of analyzing or overthinking to dismiss the painful emotions that surface from unre-solved wounds of the past. Many people who have experienced physical or sexual abuse may engage in these defenses to unconsciously stay dis-connected from their bodies which were violated.

Another defense mechanism worthy of mentioning is called *projec-tion*. Projection occurs when we (mis)attribute our own thoughts, feel-ings, and behaviors onto someone else. Our beliefs about ourselves and others is based in our own unique experiences in life, with particular emphasis on our earliest learning experiences, as these tend to be the most impactful and lasting ones. Sometimes we project more positive beliefs based on our positive experiences and sometimes we project more negative beliefs based on negative experiences. In either case, we aren't always fully conscious of where our projections are coming from.

Projection is often at play when you notice feeling irritated by a particular quality or characteristic in another person. The triggering of your irritability, especially when it seems out of proportion to the situation at hand, typically suggests that deeper feeling of embodying this quality or characteristic yourself may be surfacing—meaning there is a quality in someone else that you actually don't accept in yourself. It could also be triggering a past experience of being on the receiving end of this similar quality or characteristic from another person.

In fact, if you grew up with a caregiver who was emotionally unavailable or emotionally abusive, it is likely that you received *their* projections during times when you felt negatively criticized or misjudged. In other words, if at many times your caregiver was overly critical and implied that you weren't good enough, you were probably picking up on their own feelings about themself as not being good enough. Unfortunately, however, they were probably not aware of their projections and you were on the receiving end, internalizing their implied teachings as any developing, open-hearted child would do. And if you learn about generational trauma and how it is passed down, you will probably realize that your caregivers projected the projections of their caregivers, and so on and so forth. None of this makes their behavior okay, but hopefully it helps you begin to understand how our unconscious wounds not only impact ourselves but also others around us—especially those whom we raise—who in turn pass it on to future generations.

Repression is considered a more primitive form of denial, meaning that for whatever adaptive reason, your survival instincts caused you to bury a painful experience and never share it with anyone—even yourself. If you relate to parts of your childhood being a blur and know that at least parts of your childhood were rough, this is a likely sign that repression is at play. In case you notice becoming self-critical about not being able to remember certain parts of your childhood, it's important to recognize that repression is a trauma response intended to protect you. Trust that you had to repress traumatic experiences to survive, and that if and when you are open to the journey toward acceptance the repressed memories and pain that need to surface will come out of the darkness and into the light.

Notice which of these defense mechanisms most resonates with you, but also try to not get too wrapped up in the specific labels of your defenses so that your focus can instead be on recognizing 1) how your defenses specifically show up for you *personally* in your day-to-day internal life (and stay tuned for more tools on how to do this in the following chapter) and 2) from whom you may have learned them from. Be gentle with yourself in your explorations, remembering that these defense mechanisms are there as a form of survival. You can unlearn them through a commitment to continuous learning and effort over time. Practice self-compassion and patience as you learn the skills in this book to help you work through them. In summary, the denial that operates in many forms—numbing, dissociating, and detaching through defenses like compartmentalizing, rationalizing, intellectualizing, minimizing, repressing, projecting, or otherwise neglecting and invalidating feelings—can be considered the *opposite* of acceptance, but they are necessary to identify on the journey toward acceptance. It's crucial to note that acceptance does not mean that what happened to you was acceptable. If what happened to you was acceptable then you would not be feeling detached in a numbed-out, dissociated sort of way, or otherwise defending against difficult past experiences.

Rather, acceptance means that you have fully faced and embraced the buried pain associated with the traumas from your past that were not acceptable. It means that you have wholeheartedly acknowledged each of the unprocessed and bottled-up emotions through a willingness to remain present and engaged in compassionate inquiry with yourself. This allows you to understand and integrate the various important teachings those unprocessed emotions provide. It means you have accepted the impact of the trauma—not necessarily the trauma itself.

In other words, healing depression rooted in early trauma is really about accepting all of the feelings that the younger versions of you could not feel at the time, as well as the feelings the current you may feel when you look back. Part of accepting all of those deeply buried vulnerable feelings is identifying and working through all of the unconscious defenses and walls you've built to barricade them from being felt—and appreciating this journey toward a more understanding and loving relationship with the various parts of yourself. When thinking about acceptance as the opposite of denial, acceptance really means that whatever you were and are feeling is okay. It means that whatever you felt then and feel now deserves undivided attention, unconditional positive regard, compassion, appreciation, nurturance, and reassurance.

Acceptance, unlike denial, does not have any agendas to control or change your experience. It involves a process that allows you to touch the experiences connected to the wounded, unhealed parts of yourself with the unconditional love that your younger self never received in the first place. It means your most vulnerable self is worthy of being seen, felt, and celebrated.

The Path Toward Acceptance: EMDR Therapy Overview

In service of both the greater self-awareness required to realize acceptance and acceptance itself, EMDR therapy is arguably the most useful and optimal treatment modality for trauma-driven depression. Why? In short, because 1) it is one of the only trauma-focused therapies shown to be effective for treating depression, especially more chronic, severe cases of depression, and 2) the techniques used in EMDR therapy will purposely trigger your deepest wounds which, as you just learned, is going to simultaneously set off your strongest defense mechanisms. By the way, if you have previously learned about or otherwise heard of the buzzword "trigger," you might notice an automatic negative association with this word. If this is the case, congratulate yourself, as this shows you are building greater self-awareness, and acknowledge any automatic judgments you observe with openness and curiosity. Then, gently challenge yourself to start to associate triggers with being an essential window into your unconscious, unhealed parts, and therefore a very positive thing for your growth. Within your pain lies the potential for immense growth and strength.

In other words, anything that is triggering for you, including and especially the process of EMDR, provides rich opportunities for self-understanding, acceptance, and transformation. When you make the choice to explore what's beneath your triggers through EMDR therapy with courage and openness, it rapidly enhances your self-awareness and produces important insights about and connections to various parts of yourself. With greater self-awareness comes an ability to gain a deeper knowledge of the parts of yourself that most need to be touched and felt with love. So, seize the opportunities for getting closer to love each time that you are triggered!

EMDR, which stands for Eye Movement Desensitization Reprocessing, was developed in the 1980s by a psychologist named Francine Shapiro (Shapiro 2017). Interestingly, she spontaneously discovered the effectiveness of rapid eye movements she was making while out walking and reflecting upon a recent distressing experience. This chance discovery then motivated her to start conducting experiments that ultimately led to the initial development of EMD in 1987 and, subsequently, EMDR in 1991 to highlight the focus of a broader approach to trauma processing. To this point, it is important to understand that EMDR therapy is not simply about eye movements alone to heal from depression and trauma—it consists of a comprehensive and integrative approach that includes eight total phases. The eight phases are:

1. History taking and treatment planning

2. Preparation

3. Targeted assessment of critical memories driving current symptoms

4. Desensitization

5. Positive belief installation

6. Body scan

7. Closure

8. Reevaluation

The use of eye movements is part of a technique referred to as *bilateral stimulation*, which involves alternating between activating the left and right sides of the body. This method helps your left and right brain hemispheres communicate in order to process and regulate your emotional experiences. Visual input was the first type of bilateral stimulation used in EMDR—hence the term *eye movement*—but other sensory input such as tapping or auditory tones can alternatively or concurrently be used.

Altogether, EMDR therapy draws from and brings together various therapeutic approaches: a focus on early childhood events originally emphasized by psychodynamic therapy, conditioned responses inherent in behavioral therapy, "core beliefs" as first coined by cognitive therapy, the emotions of experiential therapies, the bodily sensations of somatic therapies, the imagery characteristic of the work of hypnotic therapies, and the contextual understanding of systems theory. EMDR aims not only to relieve the suffering that accompanies depression, but to help individuals realize their fullest potential. Now that is a comprehensive approach! What do you think so far?

Research Review of EMDR for Depression

EMDR is recognized as a gold standard treatment for PTSD (Schnurr et al. 2024) with strong evidence in more than thirty randomized clinical trials demonstrating its effectiveness in adults and children with PTSD (de Jongh et al. 2024). EMDR therapy has also shown significant improvements in low self-esteem and general psychological symptoms (Griffioen et al. 2017), which are manifestations of unresolved depression and trauma. As mentioned above, EMDR is the only trauma-focused treatment that has a growing evidence base for treating disorders other than PTSD, especially comorbid depressive symptoms that are typically assessed alongside PTSD (Boterhoven de Haan et al. 2020, Matthijessen et al. 2024, van der Kolk et al. 2007).

Clinical trials have compared the efficacy of EMDR therapy for depression against other treatment modalities such as antidepressant medication and cognitive behavioral therapy (CBT). In short, these studies showed EMDR therapy to be either equivalent or slightly superior to other treatment modalities in improving depression. Below are several examples of such study findings that may further motivate you to engage in EMDR therapy:

- Bessel van der Kolk and his colleagues (2007) compared the effectiveness of fluoxetine (the generic name for Prozac) with EMDR treatment and placebo in patients with comorbid PTSD and depression. They found that the patients who received EMDR had significantly lower depression scores than the patients who were receiving fluoxetine.

- Ostacoli and others (2018) found that both EMDR and CBT showed significant reductions in depressive symptoms when used as an adjunct to antidepressant medication, with EMDR leading to slightly better outcomes in reducing depression symptoms compared to CBT for patients with recurrent depression.

- Hase and his colleagues (2018) similarly found EMDR to be superior to medication alone, especially for treatment-resistant depression, by improving emotion regulation and processing unresolved trauma.

- In a prior study that combined EMDR with CBT and compared it with CBT by itself, researchers found that EMDR combined with CBT resulted in higher remission rates and greater reductions in symptoms of depression compared to CBT alone (Hofmann et al. 2014).

- In a trial that compared Visual Schema Displacement Therapy (VSDT) to EMDR therapy, EMDR was found to be superior to both the VSDT and wait list control groups in reducing symptoms of depression and general psychopathology—both immediately following treatment and at a 12-week follow-up (Matthijssen et al. 2024).

- In another trial that compared EMDR to imagery rescripting (ImRs) therapy for adults with PTSD due to childhood trauma, both modalities were found to significantly reduce PTSD symptoms, depression, dissociation, trauma-related cognitions, shame, guilt, and hostility, with treatment gains increasing over time at immediate post-treatment, eight-week and one-year follow-ups (Boterhoven de Haan et al. 2020).

The final research to share with you is the first-ever published systematic review, meta-analysis, and meta-regression (an extension of a meta-analysis that examines factors contributing to results), evaluating the efficacy of EMDR for treating depression specifically (Seok & Kim 2024). The results of the researchers' analyses confirmed that EMDR consistently reduces symptoms of depression with diverse populations, presenting issues, and varying session lengths, and is an effective long-term treatment for depression. Moreover, they found that EMDR is especially effective the greater the severity of the depression. Their findings corroborate previous researchers' suggestions that depression treatment should consider the influence of trauma to increase its effectiveness and reduce relapse rates (Hase et al. 2018, Yehuda et al. 2012).

Understanding Depression and Acceptance Through an EMDR Lens: The AIP Model

While EMDR therapy does not use the term acceptance per se, its underlying theoretical model, called the *adaptive information processing* or *AIP model*, similarly sees depression and other present-day symptoms as being rooted in dysfunctionally stored memories from childhood that have not been sufficiently processed. From the AIP model's perspective, trauma is defined broadly as any adverse event, no matter how big or small, that has had a lasting negative impact on the self and psyche. That lasting negative impact is evidenced by the thoughts, emotions, and physical reactions associated with the dysfunctionally stored memories that are inappropriately coloring one's perceptions and being triggered in similar present-day situations. The AIP model can help you better understand how EMDR therapy is not simply about eye movement techniques alone and is instead rather comprehensive in its understanding of the roots of depression, hence its emphasis on sufficient processing of traumatic memories. The model suggests that sufficient processing, where acceptance is needed, will help memories be functionally stored and therefore eliminate symptoms of depression and trauma.

Said in another way, your current depression is likely an *activation*, albeit typically not conscious, of your wounded past self—the innocent but traumatized child that lives on in you. This perspective has become locked in place, causing you to see the present through that similar lens of defectiveness, unworthiness, unlovability, or lack of safety or control. The unresolved past is thus still influencing the present, which you might notice at times when you have an emotional or physiological reaction that seems out of proportion to the situation at hand from a logical standpoint. The AIP model that guides EMDR therapy practice posits that the emotional aspects of these memories are not properly integrated, which validates the point covered earlier in this chapter about the apparent discord you may consciously notice between your logical mind and your emotional brain that suggests you haven't reached acceptance.

The good news is that the AIP model also emphasizes our psyche's natural propensity to heal wounds—much like our body's natural propensity to heal after a physical injury. Evidence is further provided for this by the fact that you're here reading this now! The initial goal of EMDR therapy is to help you process and free yourself from these dysfunctionally stored experiences, essentially through properly integrating the unfelt experiences of all versions of yourself between the past and present. To summarize, proper integration requires sufficient processing, and sufficient processing leads to *resolution*, which EMDR equates to acceptance.

Signs of Acceptance

This might lead you to ask, what is acceptance? From an AIP-informed EMDR therapy perspective, *acceptance* can be understood as the adaptive integration of the dysfunctionally stored memories through sufficient processing of those memories. The trauma is no longer considered unprocessed or unresolved. An indication of acceptance through sufficient processing is that the present-day situations that were initially triggering of the dysfunctionally stored memories from childhood are no longer triggering. The past is no longer being relived in the present in the form of those thoughts, feelings, and sensations centered on being defective, unworthy, unlovable, unsafe, or out of control. What has been repressed has been brought to conscious awareness, learned from, and appropriately processed such that you're living with a clearer and more secure sense of relating to yourself and others.

Again, acceptance through sufficient processing means that when you are reminded of your trauma in present-day life, you are no longer being activated in the ways you were prior to beginning EMDR. You will learn more about how to specifically gauge for acceptance during the reprocessing phases of EMDR, and you will have a clearer understanding of these concepts when you have experienced them for yourself—so if you feel somewhat confused, remember that this is normal and stay the course! Nevertheless, the most obvious indication of resolution is that when you are reminded of your trauma, you notice neutral feelings about it instead of the hodge-podge of negative thoughts, emotions, and physical feelings and sensations you had been experiencing before. You are also likely to notice a more compassionate perspective toward yourself and others in general and more specifically in contexts that had previously been triggering. You are also likely to feel more resilient, appreciative, confident, and brave for facing some of your deepest traumas. You will notice a complete shift in your experience compared to before, but in a way that happens subtly and slowly over time.

Summary

As you've started to understand in this chapter, acceptance is the ideal solution to healing from depression, especially when it's rooted in trauma that has never been fully acknowledged. Acceptance is a complex journey that often requires many twists and turns to attain the greater self-discovery that follows. When you decide to commit to this challenging but meaningful journey, you'll slowly start to bring to light the origins of the different defense mechanisms that keep you from the deeper dives into your pain needed for acceptance. You've also begun to learn that EMDR therapy is a particularly effective tool on the journey to acceptance of trauma-rooted depression, especially with its underlying theoretical model that emphasizes the need to sufficiently process the unresolved childhood trauma that is triggering your present-day experiences of depression and its associated ailments.

As with any other skill you commit to mastering, you'll come to a greater understanding of all of these concepts when you actually experience them for yourself. To this point, in the next chapter you will learn about some other important tools to start developing as you embark on your acceptance journey.

CHAPTER 3

Prerequisite Phase (0): Necessary Ingredients for the Journey

Trauma blocks love. Love heals trauma.

—Frank Anderson

You have started to understand thus far that depression has become increasingly common, manifests in many sorts of ways, and is often born out of experiences of childhood trauma even and especially if there is not conscious awareness of this. Depression rooted in childhood trauma requires acceptance, which is a complex and challenging journey requiring deep reflection and self-awareness. Accordingly, EMDR is an especially useful tool, providing space to enhance self-awareness and facilitate childhood trauma reprocessing. Remember that accepting feelings isn't about trying to control or change them, but to simply allow them to be. Thus, the attitude of self-awareness that is important for you to build is a *loving* self-awareness.

Defining Love for Yourself

To start to build this loving self-awareness, you're going to define love. Consider these questions, giving yourself space and time to reflect on them. You might write your answers down in a journal, or discuss them with your therapist or another trusted person. This exercise is also available as a free tool at http://www.newharbinger.com/56975.

- Can you identify some moments during your life when you felt loved? Notice the memories and people that come to your mind.

- What is it about these situations or people that made you feel loved?

- What are the qualities, characteristics, energies, and attitudes of the people you identified as feeling most loved by?

- How do you like to give and show love to others? Perhaps you show love through touch, through acts of service, through showing up and spending time together, or some other way. This might be similar to how you like to receive love.

- How does it feel to give love to others? Think about what comes up in your thoughts, your bodily sensations, and your emotions.

- How would it feel to show and give yourself love in the same way you give it to others? Note any thoughts, body sensations, and emotions that show up when you think about doing this.

What came up for you while doing this exercise? Take some time to go for a walk, take some slow-paced breaths, or journal about how this was for you. Show yourself gratitude for taking the time to engage in this work, as it is challenging without a doubt. After a break, come back and reflect on your answers. Look at the qualities and characteristics that came up when thinking about with whom and when you felt safe and loved. Likely, some of those included kindness, patience, open-mindedness, dependability, and a forgiving nature. You might also have paid attention to how you feel emotionally around such people: safe, warm, special, free to be yourself, and accepted in all your weaknesses and not just your strengths. Perhaps even a pet came up, as they are also loving and stable presences in your life.

What Love Is Not

This next exploration may evoke some unpleasant internal experiences, but nevertheless is also important in helping you understand what love is through considering its counterpart. As such, answer the opposite to the above questions in your journal: What are times that stick out to you when you have felt the most unloved? What qualities or characteristics were present in those people that you speculate contributed to feeling unloved? Not surprisingly, the characteristics you identified in such people in these instances are probably antonyms to the characteristics you described above. Something about their use of words, tone, volume of speech, and attitude probably stood out to you in a negative way. Alternatively, perhaps there was a complete lack of communication, kindness, and availability that stood out to you. Instances of abuse, neglect, betrayal, disrespect, humiliation, belittling, or any actions with a clear intention of causing harm to you likely came up.

Accordingly, in building loving self-awareness, you have come to first recognize what love is and what it is not to you personally. With that recognition you can start to learn to treat yourself with some of those same characteristics and qualities in others that made you feel loved and supported. You can also discern from your personal experiences that the foundation of love is understanding; in this journey you must first and foremost work to understand yourself. Simply put, understanding yourself requires deep listening and loving speech. Deep listening, which is a state of awareness that is especially lacking if you've been in a chronic state of survival, can be fostered through building the skill of *mindfulness*, and loving speech can be strengthened through the ongoing practice of *self-compassion*. Both of these two skills will increase your loving self-awareness.

Necessary Ingredient #1: Mindfulness

Mindfulness is an essential skill to start building every day as it contributes to increasing your loving self-awareness and ability to more healthily regulate internal experiences in service of acceptance. Since the process of EMDR will deliberately trigger painful emotions, thoughts, and sensations, it is especially important to have a repertoire of tools for emotional regulation upon which to draw. Aside from the education you are receiving from reading this book, mindfulness is arguably the best first step to take on the journey to acceptance. Learning to be with your present-moment experience without judgment is transformative and, when combined with deep reflection in a therapeutic space, will facilitate the understanding that is necessary to generate love and acceptance.

In the Western psychology world, mindfulness was derived from Eastern spiritual and philosophical traditions of meditation, primarily Buddhism. These traditions describe mindfulness meditation as a method available to anyone; the goal is to minimize suffering and enhance positive qualities such as awareness, insight, wisdom, compassion, and composure. Mindfulness meditation in particular is part of the eightfold path in Buddhism and is thought to help achieve self-acceptance, or *maitri*. The four parts of maitri are facilitated through meditation: commitment, awareness, willingness to experience negative emotions, and attention to the here and now.

Translating this to Western psychology, mindfulness has been defined as "the awareness that emerges through paying attention on purpose, in the present moment, and non-judgmentally to the unfolding of experience moment by moment" (Kabat-Zinn 2003, 145). As with any concept, mindfulness is best understood through continuous practice and lived experience. Nonetheless, here is a breakdown of the major components to focus on when building this skill.

The first component is *intentional awareness*, meaning when you sit down to practice the first part is a conscious choice you are making to be aware. The second part is what your intentional awareness is focused on, which in mindfulness meditation is always the *present moment*. If you are doing a breathing meditation, for instance, your awareness will be specifically focused on your breath and noticing how it flows in and out of your body with each inhalation and exhalation. If you are practicing mindfulness while washing the dishes, your awareness will be focused on the sensations you experience moment by moment as you are washing dishes. This component also involves noticing when you become distracted during your practice, whether with other thoughts entering your mind, or feelings arising moment to moment.

The third component is cultivating an *attitude of nonjudgment* in relation to your awareness of the present moment. It is about *how* you are attending to the present moment and emphasizes being with your experience without judging it. This is typically the hardest component to train, as we are hard-wired to be judgmental, problem-solving beings. We need to, for instance, be able to discern when our safety is being threatened so we can react accordingly. In the modern-day world, however, this means we may end up automatically judging our internal experiences as "bad" or "good" which might also fuel some of our defense mechanisms. The automatic problem-solving we engage in becomes a sneaky part of our defenses that keeps us from accepting our experience as it is. That is, this automatic judging mind can prevent us from accepting the unpleasant experiences that accompany painful emotions.

However, with continued mindfulness practice, little by little, we can start to become more aware of these automatic judgments and problem-solving processes as they unfold. For instance, with just a few minutes of mindfulness practice per day over the course of a few weeks, you will start to have an increased awareness of when you are feeling irritable or impatient and, as such, a better capacity to regulate this experience so that you are not reacting to it. Imagine where you might be over a longer span of time from building this healthy brain-retraining habit. You will eventually start getting to a place where you can observe your inner experiences without judging or reacting to them, which will open doors to new worlds of possibilities and cultivate a newfound sense of personal strength.

In summary, mindfulness enhances the deep listening that fosters love and acceptance because it is about being present with your experience in a nonjudgmental way. It is a different sort of way of paying attention than your default mode. You cannot necessarily control thoughts or feelings of worthlessness, unlovability, or inadequacy that enter your experience, but you can learn to become aware of them without judging them as true or false or otherwise trying to engage with them. Try it now: take a moment to look inward, and observe any thoughts, feelings, emotions, or sensations without trying to solve or control them. What do you notice, moment by moment?

Many people assume that mindfulness is about achieving a blank mind or a place of zen or enlightenment, or that you are supposed to feel calm and relaxed during or after a meditation session. The most important thing to remember about mindfulness is that the goal of mindfulness practice is *not* to achieve any sort of state, but rather to remain in the present moment without judgment. Mindfulness is about *being* rather than *doing* in the usual autopilot mode that we fall prey to because our procedural memory allows us to do routine things without full conscious awareness. For instance, remember what driving or riding a bike used to be like when you were first learning and how much more brain power it took versus now? The goal is to be here, in this moment, observing your experience without trying to alter it. If you notice yourself trying to change it, though, 1) congratulate yourself, as this is a necessary part of the process of deepening your self-awareness of your ingrained defense mechanisms, and 2) acknowledge that you are attempting to control your experience so you can shift back to the sensations in your body.

The beauty of mindfulness is that you can practice it basically anywhere and on anything. You simply choose something to focus on and start to train your mind to be aware of what you're focusing on without judgment. Many people who begin mindfulness tend to start practicing by doing a breathing meditation, using the breath as the thing to focus on. During this process, whether you're focusing on breathing, brushing your teeth, cleaning dishes, or driving, your mind will naturally wander off. You might notice yourself thinking about if you're doing this right, or other things you have to get done. You might start to feel impatient or irritated, or maybe even bored. Each time you notice becoming distracted is a moment to congratulate yourself, as this is part of the practice. You can acknowledge that you have become distracted, recognize the experience you are having, whatever its form, and gently return your attention to whatever you chose to anchor your focus on. Each time you do this, you are training and strengthening your nonjudgmental self-awareness.

You may have already noticed in the previous chapters that you have been encouraged to stop and lovingly observe any reactions you might be having to the content of this book, which may trigger pain tied to unprocessed trauma. There will continue to be pauses like this throughout this book to encourage your continued practice of mindful self-awareness; however, it may also behoove you to begin practicing this way of being in other areas of your life. Start somewhere small and realistic, like picking an existing daily activity to practice mindfully; try different activities with a mindful attitude, and do what works for you. All it takes is five minutes a day to start retraining your mind in this way. It may help to keep a journal where after each practice you can record anything that you noticed coming up; this journaling can provide further opportunities to continue learning to process your experience without judgment and be the most helpful base for getting to know yourself over time. Have fun with it!

Necessary Ingredient #2: Self-Compassion

Many of you were probably taught the golden rule when you were growing up: treat others the way you'd like to be treated. While the golden rule is certainly helpful to instill in a developing brain, what is equally if not even more helpful is being taught to treat *yourself* the way you'd like to be treated. It seems humanity would highly benefit from this teaching. In short, compassion, defined in psychology as "being touched by the suffering of others, opening one's awareness to others' pain and not avoiding or disconnecting from it, so that feelings of kindness toward others and the desire to alleviate their suffering emerge" (Neff 2003, 86–7), should start from within.

While mindfulness and self-compassion are part of the same family, self-compassion often involves a bit more action. It takes mindfulness a step further, requiring deep listening followed by loving speech to yourself. Self-compassion involves applying the golden rule to yourself and treating yourself like you would a dear friend. It can be described as having a positive and caring attitude toward yourself during moments of suffering.

In psychology, self-compassion is comprised of three interconnected elements during moments of personal suffering and failure: 1) self-kindness versus self-judgment, 2) a sense of common humanity versus isolation, and 3) mindfulness versus overidentification. *Self-kindness* is being warm and understanding toward yourself when the feelings of worthlessness, unlovability, or inadequacy that accompany your depression get triggered, rather than following those feelings down an unhelpful rabbit hole of self-loathing and self-criticism. It is about being your own best friend, especially during those moments of suffering.

Take a few moments to think about times when a close friend has come to you for support when they were struggling or feeling bad about themself. How have you typically responded to them in situations like these? Take note of the things you have said, the tone of voice in which you said them, and whatever else you may have done to offer your support. Now consider when you have struggled and felt bad about yourself, as well as how you typically respond to yourself in such situations. Do you notice any differences in how you treat others versus yourself despite the similarities in suffering? If so, gently inquire within why this might be. How might things change if you were to treat yourself the way you treat a dear friend?

The second part of self-compassion, *common humanity*, is about recognizing and appreciating that suffering is universal and part of what makes you human. This is not intended to invalidate your suffering. Instead, it is intended to help you understand that you are not alone in your suffering, so you can foster a greater sense of belonging and interconnectedness. In moments of suffering, self-compassion encourages you to remind yourself that suffering is a part of living, that other people feel this way and similarly struggle at times in life. Take a moment to put your hands over your heart as you practice turning toward and acknowledging your inner experience while reminding yourself you are not alone.

Lastly, self-compassion requires that you take a *mindfulness*-centered approach to your suffering by being fully present with and holding your painful experience without judgment so as to neither suppress it nor dwell on it. You want to acknowledge it without overidentifying with it in such a way that you end up reacting from a place of control. There is so much more to self-compassion aside from what has been covered thus far; you may benefit from visiting http://www.selfcompassion.org for more information, resources, exercises, and guided audio recordings to help you practice mindfulness and self-compassion. This chapter will end with one particularly helpful meditation practice called RAIN that encompasses the three elements of self-compassion.

RAIN is an acronym first coined by Vipassana teacher Michele McDonald and popularized by psychologist and meditation teacher Tara Brach to help you remember a mindful approach to and through difficult feelings when they arise:

Recognize

Allow

Investigate

Nurture

The first step is *recognizing* when you have become emotionally triggered. If you are not in an appropriate or safe space to deal with your emotions in the moments they arise, then you can use this exercise to bring up that difficult experience later on when you are in a safe place to address it. With the recognition that you are experiencing pain, you can congratulate yourself for becoming aware and start to acknowledge what you are feeling emotionally and how it is physically manifesting in your body. Try to keep your breath flowing in and out of your body as you attend to your unpleasant internal experience. Observe what you are feeling in your body and what thoughts are arising in your mind with a gentle curiosity. What is the name of this emotion or mix of emotions arising in your body?

Next, practice simply *allowing* yourself to have this experience, as unpleasant as it may be. This is where you want to practice being versus doing. Your intention here should be one of love and acceptance. If your intentions are to fix or control your experience (the opposite of acceptance) then this will not work—your body will be able to tell the difference when your intentions are coming from control and impatience! It may be helpful to imagine seeing that the young child in you is suffering so you can practice holding that young child and telling them whatever they are feeling is okay. You might practice saying to yourself and your emotions, "It's okay, I'm here for you. I'm listening."

With the intention to listen deeply, you can gently *investigate* this experience more, to better understand why this feeling or these feelings have arisen. Once again, the agenda behind your investigation needs to be about genuinely wanting to understand your experience rather than trying to control and get rid of the experience. You may simply ask your emotions, "Why are you here? What do you need me to know? What are you trying to communicate?" Stay patient and still as you await an answer from within, which may come in the form of thoughts, feelings, sensations, or a combination thereof. We will also be covering EMDR-specific investigation questions for this in the chapter ahead to further help with this part.

With a clearer understanding of your needs from the above steps, you can *nurture* yourself with compassion. Perhaps the hurt young child that got triggered within you needs to know that they are loved, that everything is going to be okay, that they are safe and protected, that it's not their fault, or that they are doing a great job and deserve praise for their efforts. Perhaps the area in your body that feels tight or tense needs your loving awareness and a soothing touch. For instance, you might place your hands over your heart as you allow tears to roll down your face, give yourself a warm and genuine embrace, or rub your belly to soothe the knots churning in your stomach. Picture yourself holding, hugging, and comforting the young child version of yourself. Draw from the attachment figure resource exercise in chapter 1 (also available on the free tools site for this book at http://www.newharbinger.com/56975) and picture a loving figure in your life hugging and comforting you right now. As long as the action you take is coming from a genuine place of care and you are trusting your feelings and their needs, you are doing it right. Again, acceptance is less about trying to change your experience and more about a natural loving awareness of and truly being *with* your experience.

Remember that both mindfulness and self-compassion, including the RAIN steps above, are considered *skills*. To become skilled at anything requires learning, and learning requires repetition and consistent practice over time to start to develop. Simply reading about these concepts is not enough to have an impact on your relationship with yourself, though it is certainly a great place to start. Understanding these skills will come through regular application of them during your lived experience. Using them here and there, however, is not sufficient to help you change ingrained defense mechanisms. There is simply no quick fix to these so you must persist in your practice, even and especially when you're noticing improvements. As such, these skills are just like any other and meant to be practiced daily; even just a few minutes will suffice. You've got this!

Necessary Ingredient #3: Motivation and Knowing Your Why

As you have learned in previous chapters and, most of all, through your lived experience, the path to acceptance is not for the weak of heart. It is an incredibly challenging journey. As you start to bring deeply buried painful emotions tied to adverse childhood experiences to the surface, secondary thoughts and feelings to stop following this path—typically influenced by those ingrained defense mechanisms—are likely to come up to attempt to sneakily deter you from fully engaging in the process. And while it is absolutely okay and necessary to give yourself breaks and distract yourself in healthy and meaningful ways, transcending depression and trauma are less about *getting rid* of unwanted experiences (since that is the opposite of acceptance) and more about engaging in a meaningful, heart-centered life. After all, you are seeking help because ultimately you want to live, and a big part of living life fully is simply being present.

Living in the present moment despite what your internal experiences may bring requires a certain sort of skill set, which is why mindfulness and self-compassion exercises were introduced as important tools to continue practicing and building every day. The other piece that can help drive you to both practice these skills and stay present for all parts of the journey despite the accompanying pain is a kind of motivation or *willingness*. Willingness, then, can benefit from a deeper exploration of what a meaningful, heart-centered life looks like to you. As such, the remainder of this chapter includes exercises to help you explore and clarify your personal *why* you are agreeing to embark on this difficult journey. That way, you can repeatedly remind yourself throughout this process and especially during your most painful periods ahead why you are challenging yourself in this deeper self-exploration required to reach acceptance. These exercises kill two birds with one stone because they also offer additional opportunities to practice mindfulness and self-compassion.

To start with, it's ideal to situate yourself in a quiet, comfortable, distraction-free environment. For the following exercises it is essential that you first feel more connected to your authentic sense of yourself, when you're in a state that is calm, centered, compassionate, and curious. As such, begin by silently setting the intention to feel connected to yourself. You may even wish to have your hands over your heart as you set this intention. Then, keeping your hands there, start to take several slow, centering breaths. For a few minutes, simply notice and appreciate your breath as it moves in and out of your body with each inhalation and exhalation. Practice allowing any feelings or sensations that come as you give yourself this silent breathing space.

Continue staying present, still and patient with yourself for a few minutes and notice what thoughts, feelings, and sensations arise as you deeply consider your answer to this question: why did you really decide to read a book about EMDR for depression? In other words, deep within your heart, what prompted you to seek help? Continue to practice simply allowing whatever experiences arise internally. You may benefit from writing your experience out in a journal as well so you can practice being present with your experience without judging what is surfacing. This may also mean noticing the automatic judgments your mind forms during this exercise, but without considering them as truths.

The more obvious and surface-level answer to what you want, of course, is to no longer feel depressed. If you get stuck here, try to engage in a loving self-inquiry as you attempt to dig deeper about what that would mean for your life as you look across its different domains: family, health, social or romantic relationships, education, career, community, and spirituality. Think more about what you want versus what you don't want. Think about what really matters to you. In a world where you no longer feel like you're suffering from depression driven by the traumas of your past, and instead you're perhaps more driven by love, compassion, creativity, curiosity, and joy—what's different? What do you see yourself doing more of when depression and trauma are no longer in the driver's seat of your life? What are you doing less of? Allow your mind and feelings to wander to dreams and visions for your life ahead. Don't be afraid to dream big! Feel free to consult younger versions of yourself to remember some of your biggest childhood dreams and aspirations.

The following is another journaling exercise to help you further reflect upon what it personally means for you to be living life to the fullest.

Imagining Your 80th Birthday Exercise

Imagine we have fast-forwarded to your *80th birthday party*, where you are surrounded by family and friends who are each saying something about you—for instance, the kind of person you are, the kind of life you've lived, what you've stood for across your life—in celebration of your existence to date. What would you want each of them to say about you? How do you want to be remembered by others? Who are you striving to be across your various roles, whether as a fellow human, working professional, friend, romantic partner, parent, grandparent, family member, or colleague? What are you aspiring to achieve in your life? What personal strengths or qualities do you want to develop? How do you want to impact the world around you? Notice and appreciate any reactions, ideas, thoughts, feelings, and sensations that accompany you as you go through this exploration of your 80th birthday party. Trust your process here as it unfolds, and spend as much time and thought as you need here in this important matter.

The last exploration in this chapter is called the *sweet spot exercise*. This exercise is also available as a free audio track at http://www.new harbinger.com/56975.

Sweet Spot Exercise

Bring up a memory from your life that captures a moment that felt really sweet and authentic to you: a moment of pure connection to yourself or to something or someone outside of you. For whatever reason, it just felt right. It can be something really big or small; whatever you notice coming to mind, simply trust your instinct. When you have identified the memory, go ahead and close your eyes and bring yourself back to that moment of sweetness. Remember the sights, sounds, smells, and sensations in this memory and describe each of them out loud to yourself as if they are happening now in the present moment. Allow yourself to enjoy vividly recalling this sweet moment while also making space for any feelings you have now. It is not uncommon, for instance, to notice a mix of happy and sad feelings simultaneously. Practice cherishing this beautiful mix of emotions as it speaks to what really matters to you.

As you come back to your present moment experience, allow yourself to reflect on the following questions in your journal: Overall, what was this sweet spot exercise like for you? What does this memory say about what really matters to you? What personal characteristics were you showing in this memory that contributed to this being a sweet moment in your life? How were you treating yourself and relating to others or the world around you? How can this inform your journey ahead in terms of how to live your life in the most authentic and connected ways?

Ultimately, you want to clarify what your purest intentions for this journey really are at the outset, and envision where you intend to end up—as in where your life is headed—so you can reassure yourself that you are on the right path when doubt and resistance show up. And it is not a matter of *if* they're going to show up, but *when*, so make sure you also remind yourself that these are normal feelings to have along the way. It comes back to having the willingness to persist in living the life you want *despite* the uncomfortable experiences that might accompany you on that journey. It is further important to have a general idea about your values and direction as triggered by the exercises above, because it can strengthen your motivation and willingness to persevere when the going gets rough; so make sure to spend ample time engaging with the reflection exercises above. The best motivators come from within, as in the ones connected to your sense of purpose and who you're striving to be in this world. You are encouraged to refer back to this section and your overall personal *why* when moments of doubt and resistance arise during your journey.

Summary

In this chapter you've started to define love for yourself, and you've been introduced to three very important tools to develop and refine as you work toward the acceptance needed to overcome depression rooted in trauma. The first life changing tool is mindfulness, which is learning to be with the present moment without judgment. The second tool is self-compassion, which is about being with your experience with the same sort of gentleness and grace that you'd embody when with a close friend. The RAIN acronym can be a particularly useful exercise to refer back to as you develop greater self-compassion. Both mindfulness and self-compassion are going to be monumental in helping you become more accepting of your moment-to-moment experience and, ultimately, yourself. Finally, exercises to identify and clarify your deepest values and motivations were reviewed as the third important tool in this chapter. Being aware of your personal motivations will help you to keep moving forward on the challenging but necessary journey that EMDR therapy will ultimately guide you toward.

CHAPTER 4

Assessment Phase (1):
Uncovering Your Roots

Knowing yourself is the beginning of all wisdom.

—Aristotle

Now that you've gained a deeper understanding of your depression symptoms, how they might be linked to trauma, and how to continue increasing your self-awareness through mindfulness, self-compassion, and values exploration, you're going to engage in some exercises to help you with the EMDR process. On the one hand, you may already have a clear awareness of disturbing memories from your younger years that are likely the origins of the manifestations of your depression that you wish to work through. If so, keep this list handy while remaining open to going through the exercises below. On the other hand, many of us learned to adapt to our circumstances by denying, minimizing, or otherwise burying memories and their associated pain to protect them from our conscious awareness. Given our nature to be wired to both evolve and avoid pain, it is likely to be a mix of both of these two realities—you probably remember some painful experiences, while also completely forgetting others.

In this chapter, you'll start to identify memories and feelings you'd like to work through with EMDR. The first phase of EMDR aims to help you to:

1. Identify, prioritize, and assess some of the current experiences of your depression in your day-to-day life;

2. Learn techniques to gain insight into disturbing past memories you'll target during the reprocessing phases of EMDR;

3. Identify future desired responses to the current issues, and;

4. Explore, identify, and build upon current and needed resources.

In this initial phase, you are taking a top-down approach. This means you'll start with identifying some of your most triggering *recent* experiences in life that are nudging you in the direction of EMDR therapy—the so-called top of your conscious awareness. Then, you will work your way backward chronologically through your life—toward experiences down below your conscious awareness—to help identify the dysfunctionally stored memories that these recent experiences are activating. You are taking specific information from your recent triggering events to understand in what way the unprocessed trauma that's driving your depression is being triggered. In an EMDR approach, the goal is to get all the way down to the root where the "wound" was *initially* formed (i.e., the dysfunctionally stored memory) in order to undergo the most precise and successful "surgery" ahead when we start the reprocessing phases. For example, let's say your most triggering recent experience involved an interaction with your partner, because it triggered a depression-related wound centered on a belief in your unworthiness. In EMDR we would explore the specifics about this recent experience to then identify the dysfunctionally stored memory from childhood actually being (subconsciously) triggered—let's say we identified a traumatic interaction you had with your mother when you were five years old.

Another way to think about and understand the top-down approach is to imagine your psyche as a tree, with the branches being visible or conscious, and the roots from which the branches grew typically being invisible or unconscious. In EMDR we start by looking at and exploring some of the wounds visible in present-day situations, or the so-called branches. We then explore the depth of these. Doing so will allow us to identify and address the unconscious wounds from the dysfunctionally stored memories, or so-called invisible roots, from which any branches subsequently developed. That way, no further wounded branches will continue developing because the wound has been fully addressed all the way to its root. So in the example above, sufficiently processing that memory with your mother at five years old will heal your wound around your unworthiness, thus allowing you to see more clearly in future interactions with your partner and respond accordingly.

As you are likely catching on, the first phase of EMDR covers recognizing and understanding the depth of your wounds through your most triggering recent experiences. Many people associate the word "trigger" with something negative, bad, or wrong, which can cause them to want to avoid them, because most of us have also been conditioned to steer clear of things that bring us discomfort. But you can actually learn incredibly valuable information about yourself through your triggers. They provide windows into a deeper understanding and, ultimately, acceptance of yourself. After all, emotions serve an important purpose of communicating information to ourselves and others.

In this way, you are encouraged to recognize any negative association you might have with triggers—for instance, by noticing any internal visceral reactions you may have to reading the word itself—and work to learn to befriend your triggers. The more you are willing to lean into the discomfort of them, the more you will learn that they may be your best teachers on this journey and throughout your life. Tread lightly and with some patience and courage, and don't expect perfection.

Starting from the Top: Identifying Your Depression-Related Wound(s)

Take out your journal or notebook to reflect on the following question: How would you describe your symptoms of depression and how they are currently manifesting in your life in terms of your self-care, relationships, work, or school? There are many different terms people use to label the issues they struggle with, and there are no rights or wrongs. The aim here is to identify and prioritize some of the personal problems you specifically experience and want to improve—your wounds, so to speak.

The labels you use simply need to make sense to you in the context of your day-to-day life. Try to start by making space for and honoring your own unique language and way of identifying your problems before looking for examples from others, in service of supporting your unique, creative sense of yourself. Doing so is an essential part of this whole process.

Some common ways people describe their primary issues in the context of depression rooted in trauma include the following:

- Low self-esteem or self-worth

- Excessive feelings of any of the following:

  - Inadequacy

  - Anxiety or worry

  - Anger or irritability

  - Guilt or shame

  - Numbness or detachment

- Chronic self-doubt

- Rumination

- Perfectionism

- Overly rigid or, alternatively, overly weak personal boundaries

- Difficulties with vulnerability/emotional intimacy in relationships

Current issues can sometimes be thought of as the unhealthy behaviors or habits that are engaged in *because* of underlying depression, consciously or unconsciously coping with depression through avoidance or numbing strategies. Examples tend to include different kinds of addictive activities (pornography, sex, drugs, alcohol, eating, spending, gambling, stealing, social media, etc.), obsessive-compulsive behaviors, and isolating, avoiding, or withdrawing from social or recreational activities.

If this is the case for you, consider what it is that leads you to engage in the behavior in the first place, because while you may see this as a problem—and understandably so—it is actually an attempted solution to cope with something deeper. That is, these behaviors are secondary to the underlying and unresolved depression and trauma. Do any of the examples in the bulleted list above seem to be a reason you may engage in these behaviors? Identify which symptom is the one you'd most like to work on first.

If you have a hard time labeling or even prioritizing some of the current underlying issues you experience, this is a normal experience—*it's okay*, and that's why you're here! Our deeper wounds are not always fully conscious. The possibility for confusion highlights one of the reasons why it is often beneficial to collaborate with a therapist. However, there are multiple ways to approach phase 1 based on how your brain processes things. If you are having a hard time, practice self-compassion first and foremost by acknowledging any frustrations, and reminding yourself that you're doing just fine where you are right now. Try to trust your instincts on what first came to mind, while also recognizing that the exercise in the next paragraph may be more meaningful and clarifying to you as it starts to dive into more of the specifics from your recent life.

Identifying Your Triggers

Start by identifying a few recent experiences when your emotions were triggered—perhaps starting with the recent experiences in your life that led you to read this book in the first place. Any time that you notice that your reaction seems, from a logical standpoint, out of proportion to the situation at hand, that indicates that some deeper wound is likely being triggered. Once again, it is important here to notice and trust wherever your mind is going with regard to recent situations.

To validate where your mind likely went, most people tend to find that the situations they landed on when scanning involved an interaction they had with someone else, whether a partner or romantic interest, family member, friend, group, colleague, boss, or other person in authority. Often the case is that the stronger the love is toward someone, the stronger the pain. Said in another way, it is often those we care for the most who trigger (usually unknowingly) our deepest wounds. Perhaps it took a few hours, days, weeks, or even months to look back and be able to recognize that your emotions took over and you unintentionally personalized something that was not personal, or otherwise blew something out of proportion. Or perhaps you still have yet to recognize it and feel a mix of confusion and a wish to understand.

Once you have identified two to three recent experiences that have been triggering or representative of the current issue you identified above, write these down in a journal or somewhere handy and safe. Which of these is the one that feels most representative or resonant to you now? This may be the one that seems to be the most emotionally charged or otherwise feels obvious to you personally. Again, this process is really about learning to trust your instincts. Try not to overthink which one to choose, while also lightheartedly appreciating that your mind might automatically start to do this anyway.

Working Your Way Down: Identifying Dysfunctionally Stored Memories

Now that you have identified the recent and most representative branches of your current issue, you can use some techniques to start to dig deeper. Think about the specifics of the recent experience you chose. What about that experience was the most triggering for you?

Direct Questioning

The first technique, called *direct questioning*, is to simply inquire within as to whether there have been other memories that have felt this way. Is this recent experience reminiscent of anything from your past? Do you remember any earlier times when you felt similarly?

Practice patience with yourself as you quietly ask yourself this question and await any sort of answers without trying to control what comes into your mind. It's often in stillness that the answers we seek will reveal themselves. If a memory does surface, briefly write down that memory and at what age or grade you were in. As you do this, you may notice other memories surfacing, which you may also make note of, including your age or grade at that time.

Floatback Technique

If you are not able to connect the recent experience to any past experiences, or if the past experiences you did identify did not connect to childhood memories, try this second method, known as the *floatback technique*. This exercise is also available on the free tools site for this book at http://www.newharbinger.com/56975. It involves several steps, each of which you will want to write down to reference. This method is also going to purposely trigger uncomfortable internal experiences, likely more so than the direct questioning method. As such, tread lightly and with as much patience and self-compassion as you are able. Remember that the main intention here is to help you truly get to know and understand yourself. Remind yourself of your personal *why* from chapter 3 as needed!

First, as you go back to the recent experience you identified as most representative of the current issue you are prioritizing, hold it in mind for a moment. What image from this experience forms in your mind that represents the worst part of it? What negative thoughts do you notice having, especially about yourself, as you bring it up now? What emotions are you experiencing? What sensations do you have in your body? Write these down.

Once you have identified each of these, allow your mind to focus on them simultaneously—the image, the thoughts, the emotions, and the location of physical sensations in your body. As you do this, allow your mind to float back to earlier times in your life when you may have felt this way before and just notice what memory or memories come to your mind. Again, try to just allow whatever comes into your mind without trying to control or evaluate why something is coming up. Simply trust it.

Jot down these past experiences and around what age or grade you were in. Ideally, you want to be able to connect recent experiences back to early childhood (around 4–5 years old), so if you notice memories from middle childhood and onward coming up, focus with a gentle and curious stillness on the earliest experience that arose in your mind, and as you do that try to notice any earlier memories that may arise. Continue repeating this step as many times as is necessary until no new memories are identified.

Affect Scan

If the floatback technique is not getting you connected to early childhood memories, you may opt to use a third method, called the *affect scan*. This method is more focused on connecting your present somatic or physical experience to the past. With this method, go back again to the recent experience you identified as most representative. As you hold it in mind, notice what emotions you are having right now and what you are feeling in your body. Staying with this experience gently, patiently, and without trying to control it, let your mind scan back to an earlier time when you may have felt this way before and just notice what comes to mind. Briefly record the memory or memories and the associated age or grade for each.

Now that you have identified some past experiences in childhood that are connected to the recent experience, make note of the *earliest* memory you identified, which EMDR calls the *touchstone memory*. Also, make note of the *worst* memory, as in the one that feels the most emotionally disturbing to you now, if it happens to be different from the earliest memory. The touchstone memory is the root memory, which is the one that you are going to start with reprocessing to work on your current and most pressing issue.

If you identified more than one issue or wound to work through, which is most often the case with trauma-driven depression, then repeat the same steps above to identify childhood memories connected to recent experiences of *that* particular issue. That is, for each presenting issue, go through the same sequence of identifying 1) a representative recent experience tied to that issue—you can label it problem #2, #3, etc. to help organize your experience—and 2) a hypothesized root or touchstone memory through the use of direct questioning, floatback, or affect scan methods. Once you have your list of touchstone memories associated with each particular problem, list them in order of when they happened in your life—you could create a timeline or simply a numerical list. Then, take a look at which of the touchstone memories happened *first* chronologically speaking.

It is recommended in EMDR therapy that you start with the touchstone memory that happened the *earliest* in your life—even if it is not the one connected to presenting issue #1. The reason for this is that it allows for more efficient processing of dysfunctional material and reduces the likelihood of a *feeder memory*, or an earlier memory that would block your ability to sufficiently process a memory that happened later. However, if your earliest memory feels for whatever reason like it is not the memory you want to start with and you prefer to pick another perhaps less distressing memory that you feel more ready for, then trust your instinct and collaborate with your therapist. Instead, start with reprocessing the second earliest touchstone memory in your list.

Take another general look at your list of touchstone memories you have proposed to move forward with for trauma processing. Make sure that the memories seem generally distinct from one another. Also make sure that taken together they encompass an array of experiences and attachment relationships that comprehensively color your current experiences of depression. Experiences that involved different kinds of abuse or neglect may each need to be targeted separately, for example, and it is important that each significant relationship involved (abusive or neglectful caregivers, family members, other perpetrators, etc.) is covered among these memories as well.

This list of touchstone memories, each associated with various presenting issues, represents your current overall treatment plan for EMDR therapy. Well done on your assessment thus far! Note that this list is a *working document* that will probably need revisions as you dive into deeper self-discovery. Any such modifications will be covered during the reevaluation phase (8) of treatment. The only part you need to know for certain right now is which touchstone memory you are going to start with—the rest will be determined and refined along the way.

Identifying Future Desired Responses

Now that you have accessed a host of new information in the above exercises that likely brought up things from beneath the surface of awareness, you may find yourself making connections to other present-day experiences you had not identified at the beginning. This is to be expected, since increasing your conscious awareness of these experiences will naturally lead to making deeper and more meaningful connections between the past and present. Are there any additional relevant triggering events you are now aware of, whether it be situations, people, or places in your life that bring up some of the negative reactions you identified in the floatback or affect scan exercises? Make note of these and continue to add to this list as the connections you make from your personal history continue to increase throughout this process.

Next, as you review the triggering situations in your present-day experiences that best represent your current issues, you may also wish to consider how the more healed and evolved version of you will handle similar situations that may occur in the future. How would you ultimately like to be able to handle future situations like these? Typically, EMDR will cause them not to be triggering to you anymore, and maybe that is enough for you. However, you might also gently challenge yourself to take this a step further: start envisioning the future you—the you who is perhaps more or less boundaried in interactions with others, or more confident, expressive, assertive, patient, intentional, and in control.

Identifying Your Personal Resources

The exploration of your personal strengths and resources is an especially important one. Depression no doubt has an impact on your sense of yourself as unique, special, and worthy of love and compassion. Accordingly, it is not uncommon to find this section to be difficult, and this is all the more reason why it needs to be attended to and re-attended to sufficiently. There is no growth without some pain. Consistent and intentional time, care, and nurturing are crucial to engaging with this deep inner work. Remind yourself that it's important to be patient and gentle with yourself; this work is not meant to be rushed. Continue to identify, re-identify, apply, and draw from your strengths as you are going through the reprocessing phases ahead in service of developing a more loving, accepting relationship with yourself.

The most basic question you can start exploring is, what are the personal qualities you possess that are sources of strength for you? Practice mindfulness here by nonjudgmentally becoming aware of the commentary in your mind. Notice any negative judgments without evaluating them, and instead just allow them to pass by like clouds in the sky. At the same time, also appreciate that your mind is just trying to help you despite how unpleasant or contradictory its way of helping may seem. Note any strengths you come up with, and you might also write down any negative judgments that came up to process with EMDR later.

To give an example of this, a common general experience is initially noticing a characteristic followed by thoughts about why it is wrong or problematic—the classic way instinct can be followed by self-doubt in the context of depression. For example, perhaps you notice an initial thought that your strength is in your kindness, and then you notice a subsequent thought that this makes you weak and easily walked on. Practice becoming aware of this habitual process with an observant, curious attitude rather than being controlled by the content of the thoughts themselves. Each time you are doing this, you are reconditioning yourself to be with your internal experiences in a more loving and less critical way. You are learning to enjoy your own company amongst the full range of experiences your mind and heart automatically produce. Ultimately, you are practicing and cultivating greater self-understanding and acceptance.

Below are some other related questions to add to this exploration. You might journal your answers to further reflect on these prompts (a cheat sheet is also available on the free tools site for this book at http://www.newharbinger.com/56975). Have fun with this exercise!

- What would the people in your life that you are closest to say are your strengths? Are any of these different from strengths you would attribute to yourself?

- What would current and former bosses, managers, supervisors, teachers, or mentors say are your strengths?

- When are times you have felt most alive and connected, whether to yourself or something greater than yourself?

- Who are some of your favorite people in your life, and why? That is, what are the qualities about them that you most appreciate? Hint: the answers to this last question are likely pointing to positive qualities within yourself that you might actually be projecting onto them or otherwise denying within yourself!

To enhance greater self-understanding, appreciation, and acceptance, practice remembering these positive qualities about yourself in your early years which speak to your essence. The questions that follow can help you explore this further. If appropriate and emotionally safe to do so, consult family members and friends to help fill in gaps as needed. Give yourself permission to enjoy this process, including the deeper connections with yourself *and* others this exploration is generating! It's all about remembering to be present and grateful for every aspect of this journey.

- What do you remember being like as a young child?

- Who and what were some of the people, animals, places, movies, TV shows, characters, books, toys, gadgets, concepts, subjects, and other things you were drawn to during your childhood?

- Who or what do you recall aspiring to be as a grown-up?

While many of your childhood experiences may have been traumatizing and painful, it is also equally if not more important to remember, draw out, and refer back to the positive experiences you have of yourself, even if they seem far and few between. To this point, an essential exercise to continue nurturing a positive sense of yourself is to list any and every experience—from childhood to the present day—where you had a positive experience of yourself, regardless of whether or not other people were involved. This can involve anything from positive interactions with others to moments where you felt joy, laughter, accomplishment, pride, calm, confidence, clarity, connection, love, or gratitude. There are no right or wrong answers! The more you patiently and gently focus on bringing to mind any sort of positive experience of yourself, the more other ones you may have forgotten will appear. Keep an ongoing list of these experiences, whether in a journal, Word document, or notes on your phone, that you can both 1) add to as your conscious awareness continues to increase and 2) refer back to during painful periods when you are especially in need of self-love and positive self-regard.

The questions above are but a few suggestions for exploring the internal strengths and qualities you possess, but are by no means an exhaustive list of the methods of investigation in this essential area. Use them as a starting place as well as an opportunity to practice appreciating the most important journey that you are ever going to embark upon—the one within. Try your absolute best not to rush through this process. The deeper you go in answering each of the questions, as simple as they may seem, the more enhanced the outcome will be.

Also, notice when your creative self speaks to you about what else you might do to explore strengths, and follow that voice. To further support the curious and deep parts of you, there are many resources you can search for online that can also help with your exploration; one such free resource is the *Values in Action (VIA) Survey of Character Strengths*, found on the University of Pennsylvania Positive Psychology Center's website: http://www.authentichappiness.org. This website offers questionnaires that help you identify how much you resonate with certain strengths of character and is a valuable investment in deeper self-understanding.

Identifying Your External Resources

Now that you have spent some time starting to draw out and nurture the many internal resources you possess within, it is important to recognize and capitalize on the resources outside of yourself that have helped you and can continue to help you in this process. The EMDR exercises in and of themselves can only go so far in assisting you if you do not have healthy external resources that nourish your mind, body, and spirit—especially since the reprocessing phases can be both physically and emotionally painful.

Said in another way, EMDR is a tool, just as many other resources in your life are tools to help you throughout your journey. We know from extensive research how much more advantaged people are who have resources compared to those who do not, including factors like having social support, healthcare, adequate housing, an exercise regimen, a healthy diet, quality sleep, meditation and gratitude practice, access to nature, and a sense of purpose. These are incredibly important for physical and mental health and well-being. This suggests that "therapy" is not just limited to psychotherapy—you might wish to adopt the idea that everything you do and surround yourself with in your day-to-day life is *also* therapy!

With this idea in mind, spend some time considering and listing out any and all of the people, pets, places, communities, rituals, routines, symbols, and material possessions that are valuable resources in your life *at present*. In other words, identify your other therapies! These are important to draw upon throughout the EMDR therapy process and beyond. Recall the question you answered from earlier: During what times did you feel most alive and connected to yourself? When you recall those experiences, what external resources may have been valuable to you at that time? Try to go through all the possible kinds of resources you draw upon that contribute to a sense of physical, intellectual, emotional, social, psychological, and spiritual well-being.

Note that the exploration of current and past resources might also trigger you to recognize parts of your life that may be damaging to your health and spirit, or parts that may otherwise be missing across one or more domains—for instance, many people with depression may neglect their social support or have disengaged from certain routines in the past that they found helpful. Believe it or not, this is actually a necessary triggering, and you are exactly where you need to be. If you notice feelings of guilt or shame, or thoughts surrounding not doing enough or what you "should" be doing, appreciate that your mind is forming these judgments 1) because of prior programming and conditioning, and 2) as a means of trying to help you analyze and problem-solve. Remember to be kind to yourself if you notice you are being hard on yourself for doing or not doing x, y, or z. It is understandable and often expected that when you are in the midst of suffering from depression you are not treating yourself optimally, in part because this may not have been modeled for you or otherwise taught to you. This is why resources are discussed and built upon during the very first phase of EMDR therapy. Part of the journey toward greater self-love and acceptance is starting to notice more of what does and does not nourish you so that you can slowly but surely start acting in ways that are better aligned with your goals.

So, with the intention of self-love in mind, allow your judging and problem-solving mind to come into play as you reflect upon the following: what resources are you needing more of in your life? This includes both internal and external resources. Consider each of the different domains of well-being mentioned above to help you see which are well-nurtured and which could use some more attention.

Elicit support from your higher self here by envisioning your future self and drawing upon your future desired responses you identified earlier in this chapter. What is the future, more healed and evolved version of you doing on a typical day? How is that version of you treating themself from the moment they wake up to the moment they hit the pillow, both in their state of mind and with their routines, rituals, practices, and connections to others? Sit in a neutral, silent and still presence, exercising patience as you notice what images, thoughts, and ideas naturally come to you. That vision can allow you to gently start to set realistic and meaningful individual goals in service of your physical, mental, emotional, and spiritual health.

If you are wondering where to begin, here are two thoughts. The first one is to trust your instinct of what first came to mind as needing the most improvement. The second is that, given the overwhelming science backing the positive impact exercise has on mental health—especially depression—getting your body moving is a recommended priority, especially if physical activity is currently lacking. If your spiritual health is lacking, you might combine it with physical activity by going for a brisk walk or hike to connect with nature. And, if you are also lacking social support or need accountability to build and maintain a workout regimen, you might consider the worthwhile investment of joining a gym with group classes or team training.

Summary

You are doing a great job with challenging yourself as you reflect independently on all of the deep questions embedded throughout this chapter! Take a moment to appreciate the efforts you are making by offering yourself some genuine words of affirmation and encouragement, like "I'm proud of you for your efforts" or "You're doing amazing already." Find other ways to treat yourself well for your work, like enjoying an outdoor adventure, sharing laughs with a loved one, making or buying your favorite non-alcoholic drink, or watching an uplifting movie or show. Again, use the reflection exercises in this chapter as an opportunity to trust yourself and nurture your creative problem-solving side.

The more you start to water your own unique seeds within you, day by day, the more you start growing and blooming healthily. There are no right or wrong answers as the intention is self-exploration, discovery, and growth. Your answers to the above exploration questions will not be finite—they will evolve as you continue growing and blooming day by day, month by month, year by year, and even decade by decade. And if you are wondering how you can start to develop or improve upon the internal resources you identified needing more of as it relates to your well-being, the second phase of EMDR covered in the next chapter is aimed to help you with just that—resource building to best prepare you for the reprocessing phases ahead.

CHAPTER 5

Resource Building Phase (2): Tapping Into Your Resilience

There are no beautiful surfaces without a terrible depth.

—Friedrich Nietzsche

The second phase of EMDR continues to help prepare you for the repro-cessing phases ahead by focusing on learning how EMDR works and identifying, developing, and strengthening your internal resources. This chapter divides the second phase into two parts to separate logistical preparation from skill development.

Phase Two, Part One

The first part of this phase aims to help you learn 1) a basic overview of EMDR therapy, 2) the various forms of bilateral stimulation to use for the resource development and reprocessing phases, and 3) how to apply dual states of awareness during the reprocessing phases.

Overview of EMDR Therapy

In chapter 2, you learned about the specifics of the adaptive information processing or AIP model of EMDR therapy, and are encouraged to refer back to it as needed for clarification. Since it is necessary for you to understand what you're going to be doing and why, this section is going to more concisely recap and explain the principles upon which EMDR therapy operates. The main concept behind EMDR is that when a disturbing event occurs, it can get "locked" in your brain in the form of images, sounds, thoughts, feelings, and body sensations. This then leads to you getting triggered in present-day situations that are reminiscent of that event. Sufficiently processing and unlocking these traumatic memories is the goal of EMDR, and why you identified them during the first phase.

In the third phase, you will return to the touchstone memory to ask a set of questions to activate the memory network where it is contained, and then begin sets of bilateral stimulation. These sequences of questions help stimulate the information surrounding the dysfunctionally stored memory, which combined with bilateral stimulation then allows your brain to process the experience toward resolution. The bilateral stimulation itself—whether through eye movements, tones, or touch—will reduce your disturbing emotions associated with the touchstone memory, elicit insight, shift body sensations, and restructure negative thoughts while at the same giving you a task to accomplish. Together these will result in a greater sense of self-efficacy.

One theory of why and how this process works is that bilateral stimulation mimics what is happening during the *rapid eye movement*, or *REM*, stage of sleep. REM is the stage of sleep when we are most likely to recall our dreams, and it is known to help with both emotional processing and memory consolidation. Even more interesting and relevant is that the science behind REM sleep shows that it is often compromised in individuals with depression and trauma—in part because of the way that traumatic memories get stored in the brain compared to non-traumatic memories. Thus, when performing bilateral stimulation while processing your dysfunctionally stored memories during EMDR, one proposal of what's happening is that you're rewiring how you respond to the event in your brain and integrating those memories into associative cortical networks—similarly to what your brain is doing during REM sleep.

Another proposed theory about why EMDR works is the notion that doing bilateral stimulation while simultaneously looking at a disturbing memory with a dual attention or awareness taxes or overworks your *working memory*, which is the part of your executive functioning that allows you to process and manipulate short-term information while you're performing complex tasks. The competition of this kind of dual task—inner attention to the memory along with here-and-now experience *and* external attention to the bilateral eye movements—impairs imagery, thus making the disturbing memory less vivid and emotionally charged. This in turn is thought to provide a psychological distance from the memory and thereby facilitate resolution.

The third dominant hypothesis regarding the mechanism of action of bilateral eye movements in EMDR is that they elicit an *orienting response*, which is a natural and ingrained response of interest that is provoked when attention is drawn to any new stimulus—kind of like a reflex. It involves an initial phase that has a more alerting reaction, followed by a gradual weakening and eventual disappearance of the reaction with repeated presentations of that stimulus, as long as it is non-threatening. Therefore, in EMDR the orienting response is elicited by the stimulus of eye movements, which facilitates continuous attention to disturbing memories and subsequent information processing and physical *de-arousal*, or a relaxed state.

Worthy of note here: an additional contributing factor to *all psychotherapies' effectiveness* is the therapeutic space itself. Being able to have your painful, most vulnerable experiences and associated feelings met with unconditional positive regard, love, and acceptance is healing, especially considering the history of emotional abuse or neglect your depression may be rooted in.

Continuing to build internal resources and face uncomfortable experiences within the EMDR therapy space also expands your *window of tolerance*, a term in psychology that is similar to the notion of stress tolerance, leading to the increased self-efficacy and self-confidence that make this therapy particularly successful. The learning that happens during the reprocessing phases is best accomplished when staying within this window of tolerance—when you're neither too hyper- nor hypoaroused.

Regardless of the underlying mechanisms as to how it works, which is beyond the scope of this book since EMDR therapy is comprised of elements synthesized from all of the primary psychological orientations, know that EMDR is a very effective approach that comprises a full range of neurological responses. Randomized clinical trials show that each touchstone memory is effectively processed within approximately three ninety-minute sessions or five to six sixty-minute sessions. It makes sense that people will need more or fewer sessions, depending on a number of factors. Just know that it is your own brain that will be doing the healing, and you are the one who is in control of the process.

Applying Bilateral Stimulation

As you might guess, given the term EMDR, the originally proposed way to engage both sides of your brain and body is through the use of eye movements (Shapiro 2017), though there are alternative options available if these are better tolerated. If you are working with an EMDR therapist, you will typically follow the therapist's fingers in front of you (at least twelve inches of distance from your face if in person) from side to side, and typically in a horizontal fashion so that your eyes move at least forty-five degrees past the center on each side. Your therapist may also set up sticky notes or objects on each corner of the room to go back and forth as an alternative to following their finger movements. Or, if the horizontal movements are either intolerable or you're stuck after successive sets of eye movements, your therapist might test the effectiveness of diagonal sets of eye movements by moving their hand across the midline of your face from the lower right to upper left (or the opposite). There are also different paces at which you'll perform sets of eye movements depending on whether you are accessing internal states of calm versus reprocessing disturbing content.

If you are working with a therapist via video conferencing, there are several options. One is the use of online software. To ensure that your eyes are moving sufficiently broadly, it is important that the screen is wide enough—so a smartphone typically will not suffice. The therapist may opt to use eye movements on the screen with you, and in that case, it is also important to ensure your screen is wide enough for your eyes to go past the forty-five-degree point from the center during the eye movements. Hiding or removing your self-view and "pinning" your therapist's video should help with this. If not, another option is to set up the room you are in by putting up a sticky note at the corner or edge of each wall at eye level; then, you can seat yourself in the center of the room while you are reprocessing material.

If the eye movements are not preferred due to being physically or psychologically uncomfortable, inaccessible, or you would like to add additional forms of bilateral stimulation, tactile and auditory options are effective alternatives. There really are no rights or wrongs here, so you can use your creative problem-solving side or refer to some of the following options—remember that your therapist will be helping you here. Tapping can simply be on your thighs or knees, alternating back and forth between each. It can also be tapping the desk or table at which you may be sitting. You can also put each index finger on your outer ear, specifically in front of the ear canal where your tragus is, and tap there from side to side. There is also the *butterfly hug*, where you lock your thumbs together in front of your chest so your palms are facing your chest—like in the shape of a butterfly—while patting each hand on your chest back and forth for the tapping method.

Lastly, another tactile option is to use the buzzers. If you are combining tapping with eye movements to further tax your working memory, then the directive is to follow the left-to-right tapping with your eyes. Auditory alternatives may be those used directly by your therapist in the form of snaps, claps, bells, lip pops, or other sounds that are readily available through various resources and often combined with eye movements. Again, the pacing is going to differ based on whether you are doing a calming exercise or reprocessing disturbing memories, with calming exercises having slower pacing and reprocessing involving faster pacing to help mirror nervous system regulation.

Dual States of Awareness

It is important to understand *how* you are going to be looking at the touchstone memory that you will be reprocessing. In general, your inner attention needs to be in two places, hence the term *dual awareness*: you are going to be looking at the past disturbing memory itself while simultaneously attending to your here-and-now experience. This is different from other types of therapies that direct you to relive your past experience as if it is happening in the present.

Instead of viewing the memory from the first person, imagine that you are watching a movie of your younger self and paying attention to any thoughts, emotions, feelings, and sensations you experience as you do so. Another technique is to imagine you are riding on a train and the images, feelings, thoughts, and sensations are just passing by as you observe them. Like with mindfulness, you are simply noticing your present-moment experience as you are focusing on a memory. Doing so can help you stay sufficiently detached from the memory, keeping you within your window of tolerance where you are neither overactivated nor underactivated from an emotional and physiological standpoint. Another method you can use, if you feel too overactivated, is to imagine seeing this memory in a bubble to help keep yourself appropriately detached. These visualizations can help you view your younger self through a more compassionate lens and thereby help your perspective broaden.

It is not necessarily natural to recall a memory from this third-person perspective. If you find it difficult to do so and instead can only see the memory you intend to reprocess from a first-person perspective, know that this is not uncommon. If this does occur, then you are encouraged to start with what you are seeing, even if it is from the first-person perspective. Sometimes this is an indication that something needs to be seen or acknowledged from this perspective first. Oftentimes, once the memory is continually brought up to reprocess, the perspective will shift. Try not to overanalyze why, and instead trust your brain's ability to help you process this memory in the unique way that it may need to.

Phase Two, Part Two

In the second part of this phase, the focus is on building internal resources to use both during and outside of active reprocessing. Two of these internal resources are foundational, require daily practice to develop, and were previously discussed in chapter 2: mindfulness and self-compassion skills. Specific techniques for developing additional internal resources will be taught in this chapter; you can draw upon these to help with nervous system and emotion regulation, and to promote general emotional, mental, and psychological health.

Safe/Calm State Exercise

The *safe/calm state* exercise is a relaxing or pleasant EMDR exercise that can be used with or without bilateral stimulation. This exercise is also available as an audio track at http://www.newharbinger.com/56975. It is designed to help you create a state of mind that you can use as an internal resource whenever you need to feel calm, whether that be during active reprocessing sessions or in between them. You can use your creativity and imagination throughout this exercise as you wish. You are also free to draw upon previous memories and experiences that are associated with pleasant feelings to help you.

If at any point during this exercise you notice the image or memory you draw upon starts to become associated with people or situations that provoke unpleasant feelings, then you will need to pause, take some slow breaths or a brief relaxing break, then restart the exercise and choose a different image without such an association. This exercise is one that can be done on your own or, if you prefer, it can be done with a trusted person (follow your body's cues for this) who guides you through the sequence of steps and questions below—and you can do it on each other for reciprocity if it's a loved one and not a therapist! Know that you are encouraged to come back to this exercise to create new safe/calm states throughout your journey. The more the merrier!

The first step is to have your preferred bilateral stimulation set-up prepared—you will be doing slow eye movements or another form of bilateral stimulation for any resourcing exercise that you do, including this one. This is meant to enhance the pleasant feelings that you will induce with the imagery exercise. "Slow" means your eye movements will move at a pace of about one second per side. One "set" of bilateral stimulation is considered looking to one side and then the other (e.g., looking left, then looking right; it does not matter which side you start with). Thus, each set will last about two seconds. In this exercise you will

do between four and eight sets each time before you pause to reflect on
your experience.

As a point of reference, there are no "supposed tos" in the process
when you are doing the bilateral stimulation while focusing on your
internal experience. This means trying your best to just allow whatever
is happening to happen without judging whether it should be happening
or not (i.e., practice mindfulness!). Trust yourself and try to let go of
control, while appreciating that initially when you are doing something
unfamiliar some anxiety is bound to arise. It will pass with repeated
practice and exposure. To give some common examples of what might
come up, some people notice enhanced parts of the image, increased
pleasant feelings in their mind or body, or connections to other related
positive memories when these feelings were experienced.

1. Now, close your eyes, and take a few slow, centered breaths.
    Bring to mind an image or sense that gives you a feeling of
    safety and calm. What is it, in a word or phrase? Then, take
    more time to describe what you see (clarifying and enhanc-
    ing the image). If you are alone, you may wish to journal
    what you are seeing in this image, whereas if you are doing
    this with someone, such as a therapist or trusted friend, you
    may describe this out loud.

2. As you notice and immerse yourself in the image now,
    write or say more out loud about what you see, hear, and
    feel. Then, tune in to your current internal experience.
    What emotions are you noticing? What sensations do you
    have in your body?

3. Enhance this experience by taking a few moments to con-
    tinue to focus on the image and notice any sights, sounds,
    smells, and sensations occurring in your imagination. Write
    or say out loud more about what you are noticing. Activating
    your senses, even if imaginary, both promotes and increases
    relaxed and calm feelings.

4. Now, bring up the image or sense and concentrate on what
    you are feeling and where you feel the pleasant sensations

in your body. Take a pause to allow yourself to enjoy this experience. Now, keep concentrating on those pleasant feelings and sensations as you simultaneously start slow eye movements or bilateral stimulation (i.e., about one second per movement, four to eight sets). Then pause again. What are you noticing now? As long as your response remains pleasant, continue enhancing that state with additional sets of bilateral stimulation, simply focusing on your internal experience and pausing in between each set to notice your experience. You can repeat that an additional three times as long as the state continues to strengthen. Trust your intuition on when to stop and move forward to the next step.

5. Now with this enhanced state you are in, is there a word or phrase that represents this image or sense you have just developed? Trust whatever comes to mind. When you come up with it, think of that word or phrase and notice the positive feelings and sensations you are having. Now, concentrate on those feelings and sensations along with your cue word or phrase as you simultaneously start slow eye movements or bilateral stimulation (four to eight sets). Then pause. What are you noticing now? Continue enhancing any positive states with additional sets of bilateral stimulation, and you can repeat these an additional three times as long as the state continues to strengthen.

6. Finally, say your cue word or phrase out loud and notice how you feel.

7. Now, to test the ability of your cue word or phrase to help you in times of distress, here is a slight challenge. Go ahead and bring up a very minor annoyance, maybe something that occurred earlier in the week—a one or two out of ten on the annoyance scale—but certainly not what led you to read this book. Once you bring it up, notice how you feel; notice any shifts in your body or mind. Then, bring up your

cue word or phrase and pay attention to any shifts in your experience. What do you notice?

8. To challenge you a little further, now think of an annoying incident that is a two or three out of ten. Again, notice how you feel. Then, bring up your cue word or phrase on your own, especially noticing any changes in your body when you focus on it. Most people tend to notice that the incident becomes less annoying or they feel less bothered when they can access their safe state successfully by bringing up the cue word or phrase they "installed" to be associated with it.

Container Exercise

The *container exercise* is going to enable you to build an imaginary container you can use to store distracting or disturbing thoughts, images, feelings, or memories until you decide you are ready to face them. The container exercise (also available as an audio track at http://www.newharbinger.com/56975) is not designed to permanently ignore powerful events that have happened to you; however, it is designed to help give you a greater sense of agency and control over when you choose to face and come to terms with these issues.

Your container should be strong enough to hold what you are going to put in it, and it should not be something you use in your life for other purposes (to help remove the possibility of making unnecessary associations). It should also have a door or valve so that you can determine when you want to put something in it or take something out of it. You can always change or modify it as needed. Again, take this as another opportunity to trust your intuition and use your imagination!

Now, take a moment to picture your container. Trust whatever comes to mind. No need to draw it but if you want to do this as an empowering exercise, go for it. Once you have pictured it, close your eyes, and while taking slow, deep breaths, take some time to do your best to allow anything you would like to go into your container. You can place it in, pour it in, or let it be drawn in to your container in any way your imagination wants. Give yourself as much time as you need to allow as much to go into the container as possible, remembering to slowly breathe through this exercise. Once you have completed this, make sure to take a moment to seal up your container in any way you can imagine so that you know it is securely stored.

Now, notice how you feel after having completed this exercise. Compared to before, you may be feeling more relieved, relaxed, or in control. You might also feel a weight has come off your shoulders, your mind is less foggy, or perhaps something else neutral or pleasant. If so, take some more time to appreciate that this is how you are able to feel now after successfully using your container.

Once again, consider that there may be a time and place to bring something out of the container to face it and come to terms with it— during your therapy, journaling, or self-reflection sessions, for instance. Until then, know that you can use your container to help you manage any disturbance or distractions that come up. Like with the safe/calm state exercise, come up with a cue word or phrase that you can use to remind you of your container. You might also consider writing both of these words or phrases on sticky notes to put around your room as gentle reminders.

Resource Development and Installation (RDI)

In the first phase of EMDR covered in chapter 4, you identified and explored your existing internal resources as well as those you may be needing more of for particular situations or circumstances. This resource development and installation (RDI) exercise helps you increase and apply an internal resource. It does this by having you draw upon past experiences, either when you or someone you admire has emulated this particular internal resource. In fact, while you were going through the exercise in chapter 4 that encouraged you to make a list of past positive experiences of yourself, you likely accessed these internal resources! This is similar to how RDI works, except this exercise takes it a few steps further by using both bilateral stimulation and visualization exercises.

1. Start this exercise by identifying a particular situation or challenge where you might be needing additional resources. It might simply be for approaching traumatic memory reprocessing itself, or for other challenging situations you anticipate facing, like interacting with a particular family member, friend, colleague, or boss. Just pick one to start with and then you can come back to this exercise as many times as you want for other situations as it is a very empowering one. Once you've identified the situation, set that aside for later on. We will come back to it toward the end.

2. Then, identify the resource you need as you consider managing or responding effectively in that situation. Another way to identify the resource you need is by answering this question: how would you like to be able to *feel* in that challenging situation? The resource can be a feeling like strength, courage, or confidence; it can also be a belief or an adaptive response like patience, assertiveness, or self-compassion. Trust whatever you identify and know that you will need.

3. Once you have identified the resource, the next step is to draw upon your past when you have experienced this resource in a different situation. Can you remember a time when you experienced this resource or felt this way? Practice sitting with yourself patiently as you scan back to other similar experiences. If something comes up, what is it? Write it down.

4. If after sitting with this for a while you feel stumped, identify whether you have seen this resource demonstrated by someone else. Did you watch someone else embody this resource—whether to another person or to you directly? If so, who and what was it? If not, is there a symbol that characterizes this resource—whether something in nature, a cultural tradition or ritual, or a religious figure? If so, what is it? Write it down.

5. Now that you have identified a past experience of this resource, elaborate upon it. Write down a detailed description of the experience, especially the positive parts where you or the person or symbol is embodying the needed resource, and allow yourself to be fully present as you write so you can essentially relive the feelings of this experience.

6. Once you have elaborated upon the resource, identify an image that represents it. Trust whatever image comes to mind, whether it's an image from the particular past experience or not!

7. Bring up whatever the needed resource is that you identified and your experience of it now. What do you notice feeling as you bring it up in your present experience? What emotions are you having? What sensations are you noticing in your body?

8. Enhance this current internal state by focusing on this positive experience, and what you see, hear, and notice in your body right now. Take a moment to be with your experience. What else do you notice now?

9. Prepare to use your preferred type of bilateral stimulation. Bring up the image you identified that represents this resource. Notice the feelings it elicits and where you feel those pleasant sensations in your body, and allow yourself to experience them fully. Keep concentrating on those pleasant feelings and sensations as you simultaneously start slow eye movements or bilateral stimulation (about two seconds per set, eight to ten sets). Then pause. How does it feel to you now? As long as your response stays pleasant, continue enhancing that state with additional sets of slow bilateral stimulation, simply focusing on your internal experience and pausing in between each set to notice your experience.

10. Now you are going to associate a cue word or phrase with this resource like you did during the safe/calm state exercise. Is there a word, phrase, or positive belief that represents this resource? Bring up that word, phrase, or belief, and notice the positive feelings and where you feel them in your body when you think of it now. Simultaneously concentrate on those sensations and your cue word or phrase as you start slow bilateral stimulation (eight to ten sets). Take a pause. How do you feel now? As with before, continue strengthening this positive state with several sets.

11. Now that you have fully internalized this resource, know that you can do this on your own whenever you need it. Take a moment to bring up the cue word or phrase on your own now and observe how it feels. What do you notice? You might take a moment to journal about this experience, practicing self-compassion and mindfulness as you do.

12. Finally, now that you have successfully accessed this needed resource, return to the challenging situation you identified in the first step. This next part is called *future rehearsal*. Imagine that you are in that challenging situation you identified and see yourself applying this resource you just developed. How do you see yourself managing or responding more effectively with this resource? Write this down.

13. Taking your time with this next visualization, run a movie in your head of using your resource effectively in that challenging situation. What do you notice? Ideally, you see yourself responding in the manner that you desire, for instance encountering any difficulties with confidence, grace, patience, etc.

14. If you notice a continued positive response in your rehearsal, run the movie in your head again, but this time simultaneously do several sets of slow bilateral stimulation—as many as is necessary until you can easily visualize and feel your desired response.

If you notice that you did not quite get the desired response, no worries! This is normal and why you identified it as a challenging situation. Run a movie in your head again, and as many times as necessary until you 1) find yourself responding in the way that you wish and 2) feel positive about it. Repetition is necessary in the rehearsal process—that's why it's called rehearsal. Relatedly, depending on the challenging situation itself and how many parts it entails, you may choose to focus on enhancing one part of the experience at a time before you put it all together. Once you do have the desired response, you can run the movie in your head while you simultaneously do several sets of slow eye movements to strengthen the response.

Once you have rehearsed applying your resource in the challenging situation successfully, congratulations! Take note of how the challenging situation actually goes in real life. Assuming it will end up going positively thanks in part to your preparation, add this to your ongoing list of positive experiences of yourself introduced during chapter 4, and continue to draw upon this experience in your self-reflections to keep strengthening this internal resource.

Breathing Exercises

While you may have already learned how to use the breath as a way to practice mindfulness as discussed in chapter 2, the breathing exercises in this chapter are slightly different in their intention. The following breathing exercises are aimed at helping activate your "rest and digest" system— also known as your *parasympathetic nervous system*. In this state we are feeling calm in our bodies and minds, reflected in reduced physical tension and lowered blood pressure, heart rate, and body temperature. This helps us feel more connected to compassion and creativity, and gives us better clarity for making decisions and solving problems.

When we are stressed, whether acutely or chronically, our *sympathetic nervous system*, or what you may have heard being called your "fight-flight-freeze-fawn" response, is activated. This system evolved to help humans survive when perceived threats to safety occur. In this hyperactivated state, many things are going on internally. For instance, muscles are tensed, bodies are perspiring, blood pressure goes up, minds are racing with thoughts, and breathing is shallower and more labored—all with the intention to help give us as much energy as possible to survive a threatening situation. Think about how this is useful if you're being chased by a lion.

Because our sympathetic nervous system gets activated in the face of *perceived* threat, which includes the many modern-day stressors we all experience—traffic, bills, work, conflicts with loved ones, etc.—it is often overused and chronically activated. This is especially true for those who have unresolved trauma, whose memories of the past and their associated painful feelings are frequently triggered, therefore tricking their bodies into going into survival mode when it is neither necessary nor helpful. In fact, many physical, mental, behavioral, and emotional ailments are caused by the chronic overactivation of this system.

Therefore, learning and practicing ways to deactivate this system cannot be stressed enough (pun intended). Turning your attention inward to promote the deep and slow breathing that comes from your belly rather than your chest is the most basic method that can help you both deactivate the stress response and increase your stress tolerance. In order for these exercises to be effective in the long run *you must practice them as a part of your normal routine rather than only practicing them when you are acutely stressed.* Building a habit of this deliberate way of breathing—even just five minutes a day—will make it more automatic with continued practice over time. This means that when you are in a less conscious, more primitive state of survival you will be better able to kick it into gear effectively.

Starting with just a few minutes per day is sufficient; if you are willing to practice more than once a day, go for it. You might pair it with an existing part of your morning, afternoon, or evening routine to help you build the habit. Being consistent as you start to build a new habit is most important, so pick the time of day that is most realistic for you. Building habits also takes time, so practice being patient and gentle with yourself during the process of making this a habit. Expect that you may forget or otherwise struggle to start up a consistent routine, and take this as a learning opportunity to practice self-compassion and identify potential barriers. Trust yourself on overcoming barriers, and also know that using sticky notes, relying on app and phone reminders, and eliciting support or accountability buddies are often helpful tools.

As for the exercise itself, if you have not practiced diaphragmatic or belly breathing exercises before, you may benefit from first trying this while laying down on your back. If this is not accessible to you, it is also fine to do this seated, preferably in a balanced posture with your feet uncrossed and flat on the surface below you. Place one hand on your chest and the other on your belly so that you can gauge which hand is moving the most; ideally the hand on your belly, which should be expanding on your in-breath and deflating on your out-breath. Diaphragmatic breathing is similar to the kind of breathing you experience when you yawn—and by the way, yawns are helpful in preparing us for sleep because they relax us by activating our rest and digest system! The more challenging you find this exercise, the more you are going to really benefit from learning it.

There are a myriad techniques and options as far as the length of each inhalation and exhalation—the slowness of your breathing and the length of your exhale are most important as they help to deactivate your sympathetic and activate your parasympathetic nervous system. It is generally helpful to inhale through your nostrils and exhale through your mouth if feasible. Expose yourself to multiple methods, trust the ones that feel best for you personally, and follow your intuition on the length of your inhales and exhales.

Boxed Breathing

A great exercise to start with is *boxed breathing*, where you inhale, pause, exhale, and pause again, all for an equal number of counts. A free audio track for this exercise is also available at http://www.newharbinger.com/56975. Boxed breathing is usually done with four counts for each but you can modify this as you get into your own rhythm of paced breathing. It is called boxed breathing because you are essentially forming a box with the same length for each of the four parts—inhale for a count of four, pause for four, exhale for four, pause for four, and so on. Going slightly outside of the box method, you can also modify this to have a longer exhale compared to the length of your inhale and pauses—for instance, inhale for four, pause for four, exhale for eight, pause for four. Again, the goal of diaphragmatic breathing is to activate your parasympathetic response to relax you, and in your initial practice you are likely to be pretty focused on this deliberate way of breathing. With time, however, you may notice your mind wandering; this is where you can also fold in mindfulness practices such as clouds in the sky from chapter 4.

Grounding Exercises

Across your life experience in general and especially during the reprocessing sets, it is most helpful to stay within your *window of tolerance*, during which you are neither too over- nor underactivated as you are processing past experiences. In other words, you want to be able to maintain dual attention during the process and examine your reactions in the past and present moment. Because the experiences you will look at will be triggering, however, you can expect there to be times when you go out of that window and into a more primal state of survival. Oftentimes this is a necessary part of your process if your younger self needs you to relive something in order for it to be acknowledged. The more repeated or chronic your trauma history is, the smaller your window of tolerance is likely to be—depending on how much inner work you have already done up to this point to increase your regulation abilities, which expands your window of tolerance.

Being in an overly activated state manifests as feeling very overwhelmed, panicky, enraged, having racing thoughts, or being hyperalert to your surroundings, whereas being in an underactivated state may look like shutting down, freezing, suddenly feeling extremely fatigued, tired, numb or disconnected, or not being able to think. The more you can become aware of when you go into these altered states, the more you can take back control by using them as opportunities to practice regulating yourself.

Engaging in mindfulness and self-compassion exercises daily, and when your mood is relatively neutral, will also help increase your stress tolerance. The following exercises are simple grounding techniques to help reorient you back to the present when you have become hyper- or hypoaroused. Each of these helps you shift from an emotional to a cognitive, perceptual, or sensory focus that grounds you back in reality and a sense of safety. Try them in incremental order.

1. Reorient to breathing and posture: If you find yourself overactivated, notice your breathing and try to gently slow it down. Then, while maintaining this slowed breathing, try to take deeper breaths from your belly or diaphragm rather than from your chest. Lengthen your spine and notice the contact of your backside with your clothing and with the surface below you. Notice the contact of your socks or shoes with your feet, or the contact of your feet with the surface below you.

2. Compare textures: Feel the surface of the couch or chair you are on, and describe it. Do the same with feeling your feet on the floor, the clothing on your skin, or other textures you may be in close physical contact with.

3. Toss soft objects: Play "catch" with a soft object, such as a small pillow, stuffed animal, or balled-up tissue.

4. Work against gravity: Depending on your physical abilities, stand up and raise your arms above your head, and move your arms up and down as if you are flapping wings. Or, rise up onto your toes, or do deep squats or knee bends.

5. Do simple math: Create a task here that is challenging enough to grab your attention but without being overly difficult and therefore frustrating. For instance, count up by threes or fours, or do the same counting down.

6. 5-4-3-2-1: Engage your senses by attending to what's around you. Identify and describe five things you see around you. Then identify and describe four things you can touch, three things you can hear, two things you can smell, and one thing you can taste. If needed, go back to the beginning and identify new items for each of the senses.

If you have worked through these strategies and still do not feel grounded or regulated, use the container and safe/calm state exercises to further help stabilize yourself.

Summary

Congratulate yourself for making it through this skill-heavy chapter. You've done so much already and you're doing great! The second phase of EMDR is both an incredibly important phase and an ongoing one, as building and drawing upon the skills and techniques to help keep yourself safe and stable are foundational for not just the particularly painful reprocessing phases ahead, but for your overall health and well-being. The term *skill* itself serves to remind you that ongoing practice is required, and thus an attitude of openness to continued learning and growth is key. Your window of tolerance will continue to expand with your efforts and willingness, so remember to draw upon your personal *why* as much as needed.

As such, from a place of gentleness, self-compassion, and a growth-oriented mindset, consider this phase to always be incomplete, in the sense that as you move through life's many challenges, there will be always room for greater emotional, mental, and psychological growth. Call it a dance you're navigating between accepting yourself exactly as you are while encouraging yourself to keep growing into your most empowered, resilient version of yourself.

CHAPTER 6

Target Assessment and Desensitization Phases (3–4): Awakening Your Roots

I said: What about my heart?

He said: Tell me what you hold inside it?

I said: Pain and sorrow.

He said: Stay with it. The wound is the place where the Light enters you.

—Rumi

Now that you have bravely explored and identified a root memory or set of root memories to reprocess from phase 1, and have expanded and built upon your internal resources from phases 1 and 2, you are ready to enter root memory network territory that phases 3 and 4 encompass. More specifically, the third phase of EMDR aims to help you appropriately access the memory network where the *touchstone memory* is located, which you identified from your exploration in the first phase of EMDR (chapter 4). It also uses subjective measures for you to reference during the process so that you can gauge when to move forward with each phase. Phase 4 then follows immediately after the completion of phase 3 to begin the touchstone memory reprocessing. Therefore, be sure you fully understand both phases 3 and 4 so you can go right into phase 4.

Phase 3: Target Assessment

Since the third phase is a more targeted assessment you are likely to spend less time getting through it compared to the first phase, and you will be going directly into reprocessing with bilateral stimulation once you have completed it. As such, make sure to have both your environment and your general psyche set up for reprocessing ahead. The sequence of sections covered in this target assessment phase include:

1. Labeling the target memory

2. Instructions for reprocessing

3. Identifying the worst image or part

4. Identifying the current negative belief associated with that image

5. Identifying a desired positive belief associated with the image

6. Identifying emotions associated with the image and negative belief

7. Identifying the current level of disturbance associated with the memory

Labeling Your Target Memory

As you recall from the first phase, you have decided to reprocess the *touchstone memory* you identified earlier on to help you with your current issues. In order to refer to this memory later, since it will take multiple sessions to reprocess over time, EMDR suggests giving it a neutral label. Use this as another opportunity to trust your instincts and not overthink—but also practice appreciating your mind for overthinking if it does this anyway by observing any immediate thoughts or judgments with a playful curiosity. Examples could be more broadly the age you were or the year of this memory, or a particular aspect tied to the memory that seems significant to you like the location, setting, occasion, or topics involved.

Instructions for Reprocessing

After you go through the sequence of sections in this chapter, the touchstone or target memory is considered to be activated. Accordingly, after the memory is activated, you will be starting sets of bilateral stimulation. The pacing will be considerably faster for the reprocessing phases compared to what you practiced during the resourcing phase—as fast as you can tolerate. Each set will also be longer in duration in the reprocessing versus resourcing phase—around thirty to forty instead of four to eight sets.

Similarly to the resourcing phase, in between each set of eye movements you will be taking a pause to express whatever you are noticing during your experience—whether to your therapist or a trusted other if they are with you, or to yourself through journaling. Sometimes you will notice things change from set to set, though sometimes things won't change. For instance, your mind might go through the memory itself looking at it through various lenses, it might make connections to other memories in your life, it might start feeding a stream of thoughts or interpretations that you follow, or it might be more focused on sensations entering and moving through your body.

There truly are no rights, wrongs, or "supposed tos" in the process. Your role is to exercise mindful awareness during this process, simply noticing and giving feedback as to what is happening without judging whether it should be happening or not. This means noticing the judgments your mind might form and allowing them to pass without trying to change them. Essentially, this is an opportunity to practice trusting yourself and letting whatever happens happen. You are the one in control of the process, so just remember that if at any point you wish to stop, you get to call the shots on that. This seldom happens, but it's a precautionary measure to help you remember that you're the one in control. You can agree upon a signal to use in collaboration with your EMDR therapist so that there is a clear indication of when you wish to stop.

Identifying the Worst Image or Part

You are now going to be asked to start looking back at the memory, and as such this is a gentle warning that some unpleasant experiences are going to be triggered. Remember that this is an intentional triggering that is necessary to promote your emotional healing and growth. Much like getting physically stronger, there is not going to be any gain without the experience of pain. If needed, remind yourself of your intentions for doing this challenging albeit meaningful work as reviewed in chapter 3. Use this as an opportunity to practice strengthening mindful and self-compassionate awareness.

When you look back at the target memory in this moment, what picture in your mind's eye represents the worst part of this experience? Notice that the question is not what was the worst part of it during the time period of the memory itself. Instead, it asks you to scan through this memory and notice what image comes to mind that represents the worst part of it *right now* as you reflect on it. Sometimes it is the same as what the worst part was then, but sometimes that is not the case. Trust your instinct of whatever image associated with the memory formed in your mind. If you are having any trouble forming an image, then instead consider what the worst part of the memory is now as you recall the experience. Sometimes this process elicits senses other than the visual one and that's okay, too. Either way, record your result.

Identifying a Negative Belief

Now that you have identified the worst image or part of the memory as you think about it in the current moment, the next step is to identify a negative belief, also known as a self-limiting belief or a *negative cognition* associated with it. What words go best with that picture or sensation that express your negative belief about yourself now? Again, remember that dual attention is needed here. You are looking back at this memory and identifying what negative thoughts, particularly about yourself, you may be having right now as you identify the worst part of it. The negative cognition you identify here is typically irrational and distorted despite emotionally feeling true; it is self-referencing versus descriptive or other-focused, and is generalizable. It might be similar in language to your primary presenting issue or it might be different.

The guidance, as always, is to trust what instinctively comes to mind, and to engage in additional self-inquiry or self-dialogue as needed to get to a negative self-belief. This might be simply asking yourself what is beneath the statement you are making, as in what does it say about you as a person now, or how does what happened make you feel about yourself? State what you think of yourself in your worst moments, even if you logically know it isn't true. It is better to go with your own style of language and to show trust and respect to your instinctive voice. That way, EMDR will be more effective in helping you transform your self-limiting beliefs and feelings.

It is not uncommon to need additional guidance or confirmation here. Below is a list of common negative and opposing positive cognitions others identify that may either affirm the language you instinctively chose, or be evocative if you could not find the words to describe your experience of this memory. EMDR has divided these cognitions into four themes:

1. Responsibility (subdivided into defectiveness and action)

2. Safety/vulnerability

3. Control/choices

4. Connection/belonging

Pay attention to your body when you are reading the following list and, as you consider the target memory, notice which statement elicits the biggest charge in your body, as that is indicative of a statement that clearly resonates with the unhealed parts of you.

THEME/CATEGORY	NEGATIVE COGNITIONS	POSITIVE COGNITIONS
RESPONSIBILITY: DEFECTIVENESS Self-Worth/Shame	I am bad. .... I am unlovable. .... I'm not good enough. .... I am incompetent. .... I don't matter. .... It's my fault.	I am good. I am lovable. I am good enough. I am competent. I do matter. It's not my fault. (I'm innocent.)
RESPONSIBILITY: ACTION Action/Guilt	It's my fault. .... I should have done something. .... I am unforgiveable. .... I am a horrible person. .... I'm inadequate/weak.	I learned/can learn from it. I did the best I could. I can forgive myself and move on. I'm okay, in spite of my mistake. I am adequate/strong.
SAFETY/VULNERABILITY	I am vulnerable. .... I am going to die. .... I am not safe. .... I can't trust anyone............................... I'm in danger.	I can (learn to) protect myself. I survived. I am safe now. I can choose whom to trust. It's over, I can move beyond it.
CONTROL/CHOICES	I am helpless/powerless. .... I'm trapped. .... I am not in control. .... I can't handle it. .... I am out of control. .... I cannot trust myself/my judgment	I have choices now. I'm free. I'm in control now. I can handle it. I'm in control of my reactions. I can (learn to) trust myself/my judgment.
CONNECTION/ BELONGING	I can't connect. .... I don't belong. .... I am invisible. .... I'm different, and that's not okay. ...... I'm alone.	I can connect/I am connected. I do belong/I worthy of belonging. I deserve to be seen. I am myself/unique, & that's okay. I'm not alone. (I'm connected.)

Reprinted with permission from the EMDR Institute.

Identifying a Positive Belief

As the table above foreshadows, the next step is to consider what you would like to believe about yourself instead when you bring up your worst image or part of the target memory. This is what EMDR refers to as the *positive cognition*. It is included in phase 3 to help you consider how you would ultimately like to be able to look back at yourself when you recall this memory. It should be the most powerful statement you can think of, even though it may be hard for you to believe it at the present moment. From a bigger picture standpoint, you will want to look back through a lens of compassion while also being realistic—so you're not choosing a positive cognition that indicates an attempt to rewrite your personal history, which would suggest a lack of true acceptance and integration of this experience.

The positive cognition is an empowering self-assessment that incorporates the same theme or personal issue as the negative cognition but with implications for a positive future. Sometimes the positive cognition you identify is directly opposite to the negative cognition that you just identified, as in the above table, but sometimes there is another statement that resonates more with you or is otherwise more realistic. Again, trust your instinctive voice and try to use the language that resonates best with your mind and body. Also, try not to overthink this one too much as we will actually set it aside and come back to it at the start of phase 5, during which you will "install" this positive cognition after removing any and all disturbances associated with the target memory. During that time the positive cognition can be refined as needed.

Before setting it aside until phase 5, next you are asked to identify what EMDR calls the *validity of this cognition*. That is, when you bring up the worst image or part of the target memory, how true does this positive cognition *currently feel* to you on a scale from 1–7, where 1 feels completely false and 7 feels completely true? Notice here that you are being asked to identify how true you *feel* it is versus how true you *think* it is. On a logical level it may seem relatively true to you, but on an emotional level, right now it is likely to not feel very true. At this point in the process this discrepancy is normal and the reason why you are engaging in reprocessing.

Said in another way, the adult part of you knows it is more realistic, whereas the young child in you is wounded and feels differently. It takes time for our emotions to catch up to logic and reason, especially when depression and trauma are involved. With that being said, you probably identified a lower number on that scale. One of EMDR's objectives is to increase the validity of the cognition to a 6 or 7 during phase 5. Write down your negative and positive cognition, along with your current validity number.

Identifying Emotions

Now go back to the worst image or part of the target memory. When you recall it now, along with the negative cognition you identified earlier, what emotions do you feel? Notice what emotion you first identify, and any subsequent emotions. As a reminder, there are no right or wrong answers in this process. It is simply about noticing your experience and then verbally expressing or journaling the emotions coming up without judging them.

Depression and trauma healing are going to provoke a full range of emotional experiences, including your defense mechanisms, and you are going to benefit the most by expecting this to be integral to the journey toward acceptance. It will also be helpful to know how to identify the multiple emotions that can get triggered simultaneously, as it relates to optimal emotional regulation and processing. In general, depression is typically accompanied by feelings of guilt, shame, helplessness, fear, anxiety, anger, irritability, or sadness. The exact strength of the feelings will vary depending on your defense mechanisms; for instance, as discussed in chapter 2, many people with depression have adapted by numbing or detaching from their emotions. With continued mindfulness practice and EMDR therapy over time, those defense mechanisms can shift—they likely already have started to for you if you have come this far!

In summary, it is important to know how to identify the emotions you are experiencing. This means being able to discriminate between different emotions in terms of how they are experienced differently in your body and mind. While it seems quite basic, it is a crucial directive to include because many people were not taught to attend to their emotional experiences—especially if they experienced abuse and neglect. This is why mindfulness was discussed early on as one helpful tool for building better awareness and emotional regulation. You may also start to increase your emotional self-awareness by running through each of the basic emotions—sadness, fear, joy, love, anger, guilt, shame, disgust, shock—and asking yourself how you physically or behaviorally know you are feeling each of them. Write these down in your journal.

The more you can understand and discriminate between various emotions, the more you can come into a secure sense of who you are and what you stand for. Why? Because emotions exist to *communicate* to us and others around us about what is and isn't important. Sadness typically communicates a loss of something significant, and therefore teaches us about what is valuable to us. Guilt typically communicates that we violated our moral code of conduct with a certain action, and therefore teaches us our core values and who we strive to be in the world so we can course-correct moving forward. Fear alerts us to danger and threats to our safety and security, and anger communicates an injustice that we wish to fight against to protect what we deem is right.

Identifying Current Level of Disturbance

Now that you have brought up the worst part of the target memory, your negative cognition, and current emotions, you are going to identify how disturbing the memory feels to you currently using what EMDR calls the *subjective units of disturbance* or *SUD* scale. On a scale from 0-10, where 0 is no disturbance or neutral and 10 is the highest disturbance you can imagine, how disturbing does the memory feel to you now? If you identified a number of different emotions above, only give the SUD rating on the total disturbance you feel rather than a SUD rating for each separate emotion. As you may guess, another one of EMDR's objectives is to reprocess the memory until it is a solid 0 out of 10; that will also be an indication that you are ready to move onto the next phase.

Identifying Body Sensations

The final step in phase 3 after identifying your initial SUD rating is to ascertain the location of any body sensations you are experiencing at present. Where do you feel that disturbance in your body? Do not go into detail about the sensations at this moment; simply recognize where they are located in your body. Take note of your SUD and where you feel it in your body in your journal. Proceed to phase 4 immediately from here.

One of the therapeutic goals of EMDR therapy is to gain greater access to physical sensations and emotions so that sufficient processing and integration of dysfunctionally stored memories can be achieved. However, many people have learned to psychologically separate themselves from their bodies and may need additional sensation awareness training. Again, this is why starting a mindfulness practice and developing internal resources like the calm/safe state exercise—discussed in chapters 3 and 4—are essential prerequisites to the reprocessing phases of EMDR. This way, there is an ability to detect and appropriately tend to the body's responses to trauma. Here are some brief exercises to help you tune to responses in your body, which will also further help increase your emotional self-awareness:

1. Close your eyes and notice how your body feels. You'll be asked to think of something, and as soon as you do, just notice what changes in your body. Remember the goal here is increasing awareness of sensations in your body in response to certain cues.

2. Picture a lemon. Imagine yourself slicing that lemon in half, then again in quarters. Take one of the quarters and bite your teeth into it. Notice your body's reaction and where you feel it. (Usually, people feel an instant reaction in their mouth upon thinking about biting into a lemon. Pretty powerful what the imagination can do, right?).

3. Picture hugging one of your favorite people. Notice how your body changes and where those changes happen in your body.

4. Now, think of your target memory. Notice what changes in your body. Now, add the words of your negative cognition. Notice what changes in your body.

One final note on body sensations: if you identify with feeling either numb, blocked, or separated, you may assume that this means you have an absence of feelings throughout your entire body. Rest assured that this is actually not the case. Gently close your eyes and self-inquire as to where in your body you are noticing feeling numb, blocked, or disconnected. Wait patiently in stillness for a response from your body, then focus your attention on the location that communicates to you.

Phase 4: Desensitization

With completing the sequence of steps above in phase 3, you are now ready to begin the *desensitization* phase. Desensitization means that with repeated exposure to a disturbing memory over time, any distress that is initially associated with it will reduce. The reduction of distress associated with a memory will also allow you to look at and relate to it from a different lens than before. The lens typically transforms into one that is more neutral as a result of becoming aware of and working through any blocks to expressing deep pain and grief needing acknowledgment in order to find acceptance, as discussed in chapter 2. Overall, the desensitization process subsequently allows you to be able to see a situation with more compassion and clarity.

The desensitization phase is typically the longest since it is where the bulk of the reprocessing occurs. Remember that randomized clinical trials of EMDR show that each target memory is typically reprocessed within three ninety-minute sessions or five to six sixty-minute sessions. Accordingly, pace yourself rather than trying to rush through this part! The more time and depth you devote to it and the lesser the sense of urgency with which you approach it, the more deeply you are going to benefit.

As mentioned in phase 3, make sure to have both your environment and psyche prepared for what's ahead. Refer back to the instructions for reprocessing in this chapter and from phase 2 in chapter 5 as needed. You need to be completing the reprocessing phases with an EMDR therapist. The pacing of bilateral stimulation you will do in this phase will be faster—as fast as you can tolerate. The duration of the eye movements before you pause to process your experience will also be longer—between twenty to forty sets of bilateral stimulation depending on your individual response. After these sets, you will be instructed to first *take a breath and let it go* before you are then asked *what are you noticing now?* to encourage you to verbally process or record what you noticed. Then, once you've paused to process your experience, you will be told to simply *go with that*, restarting the bilateral stimulation for a sequence of twenty to forty sets and then repeating the following sequence of taking a breath, letting it go, processing that experience, and going with that.

Reprocessing the Target Memory

Now that you have identified all of the material necessary to activate the relevant memory network, you are going to start reprocessing the memory. Take your time with this and plan to spend only between twenty to sixty minutes per session of reprocessing the memory rather than trying to tackle it all at once. To do so, *bring up that picture or worst part associated with the touchstone memory, the negative belief you identified, notice where you are feeling it in your body, and allow it to go wherever it needs to go* as you start fast-paced bilateral stimulation for twenty to forty sets.

Take a breath, let it go. What are you noticing now? Typically, new images, thoughts, and feelings will emerge in this process; you should not try to hold on to the image with which you started as its purpose is to serve as an initial focal point to enter your memory network. Once you have expressed or recorded your experience, whatever it may be, *go with that*—meaning stay with whatever you just verbalized noticing from the previous sets of bilateral stimulation—as you start a subsequent sequence of fast bilateral stimulation for between twenty to forty sets, adjusting the exact number of sets based on your individual response. *Take a breath, let it go. What are you noticing now?* As long as you continue to notice changes from sequence to sequence, no matter how big or small they are, *go with that* as you start another twenty to forty sets of bilateral stimulation. If you get nothing, go back to the incident—*when you think of the memory now, what do you get?* Notice any shifts in perspective, image, emotions, or sensations, and *go with that* as you start another cycle of twenty to forty sets of fast bilateral stimulation.

Keep repeating this sequence over and over, pausing to take breathers, noting your experience, and doing as many sets of bilateral stimulation as necessary. Note that this part of the phase typically takes multiple sessions of reprocessing, as this root memory likely has 1) many channels of association tied to it across childhood and adulthood experiences, and thus 2) many unprocessed emotions, words, sensations, and other experiences needing full expression and deeper understanding to gain acknowledgment, understanding, and acceptance. Between twenty to forty sets is average, with highly emotional responses typically demanding forty or more sets for processing.

With that being said, even though it seems like it is just one memory you are reprocessing, it actually isn't—it's the initial memory of a myriad of connected experiences. There is *a lot* to process, and staying within the window of tolerance ideal for reprocessing means that your system can only process so much at once. Practice patience and self-compassion, draw upon your resources during and in between reprocessing sessions, and remember to trust yourself and your process. You've got this!

Returning to the Target Memory

If you stop noticing any changes for two consecutive sequences of twenty to forty sets, *return to the target memory.* When you bring up the memory as you experience it now, what do you notice? Express or record your experience, and *go with that* (whatever you verbalized) as you start fast bilateral stimulation for between twenty to forty sets. *Take a breath, let it go. What are you noticing now?* Express your experience, and *go with that* as you start fast bilateral stimulation again for between twenty to forty sets. Continue to repeat this sequence—twenty to forty sets of fast bilateral stimulation → pause to *take a breath, let it go* → express your experience → *go with that*—as long as new information is being produced.

Checking Your SUD Level

If, when you return to the target memory, you notice it seeming neutral or you notice no changes in your experience after two consecutive sets of bilateral stimulation, you are going to reassess your SUD level that was first assessed during phase 3. *When you bring up the memory as you experience it now, on a scale of 0 to 10, where 0 is neutral or no disturbance and 10 is the highest disturbance you can imagine, how disturbing does the memory feel to you now?*

If your SUD is greater than 2, *go with that* as you start fast bilateral stimulation for twenty to forty sets. If your SUD is 1 or 2, *where do you feel that in your body? Go with that* as you start fast bilateral stimulation for twenty to forty sets. In either situation, go back to repeating the sequence (i.e., the "Reprocessing the Target Memory" section above) as long as new information is being produced.

If your SUD is a 0, *go with that* as you start at least one sequence of twenty to forty sets of bilateral stimulation. *What are you noticing now?* As long as it remains neutral and you are not noticing changes, proceed to phase 5.

Abbreviated Phases 7–8: Closing and Resuming Reprocessing of the Target Memory

Again, the desensitization phase can occur over a handful of sessions per target memory and it is best to not spend more than an hour on each reprocessing session to maintain an appropriate window of tolerance and to best facilitate information processing. Although closing and resuming reprocessing sessions are parts of phases 7 and 8 respectively, they are briefly included below to easily access and reference. See chapters 7 and 8 for more detailed information about procedures for the closure of the session and reopening a subsequent session.

To close up each reprocessing session, check in with how you are feeling throughout your mind and body. Consider drawing upon the container exercise you developed in phase 2, followed by shifting your state to a calmer place if needed by bringing up the cue word or phrase and image you developed for the safe/calm state exercise. Praise yourself for the efforts you put into reprocessing, and record a positive summary of what you learned or gained from the session. Lastly, despite the fact that you stopped actively reprocessing the memory, understand that the processing may continue after the session over the course of the next few days. This means you may notice spontaneous insights, memories, physical sensations, or dreams. Briefly record, and communicate to your therapist if applicable, anything that does come up.

Each time you do resume reprocessing the memory for a new up-to-sixty-minute session, instead of going through all of phase 3 again, you will go through the following abbreviated version:

1. Bring up the memory you have been working on. What is the image that represents the worst part of it *now?* (Sometimes the worst part shifts, sometimes it doesn't. Remember, there is no right or wrong in this process. Simply notice what comes up and trust yourself!).

2. What emotions are you experiencing *now?* On a scale from 0–10, where 0 is neutral or no disturbance and 10 is the highest disturbance you can imagine, how disturbing does the memory feel to you *now?*

3. Where do you feel it in your body?

4. Now, bring up the experience, the emotions and sensations you're having now, and let it go wherever it needs to go as you start a set of fast bilateral stimulation. Then repeat the sequences in the "Reprocessing the Target Memory" and subsequent sections above.

Closing Thoughts: Reprocessing in the Context of Depression

As a reminder, there is no right or wrong way for how exactly the reprocessing sessions should go, and you are encouraged to trust your brain's natural ability to heal itself in the unique process that it does so. During the reprocessing sets you may sometimes find your mind making connections to other past or present-day memories, analyzing situations, experiencing intense emotions or sensations, drawing blanks, or not noticing changes at all. Your defense mechanisms will arise as a form of resistance to gain insight into, which is an inherent part of everyone's process of deepening self-awareness. Try to remember to stay fully present during your journey so you can appreciate all that it has to offer for your enhanced self-discovery and growth. Every part of this process is meaningful—even and especially the painful parts! Although the reprocessing associated with the target memory you selected is going to have its own unique course for you, this section aims to describe some of the common experiences you may expect in the context of depression.

There is an immense amount of grief to be expected in this journey. In short, where there is depression driven by trauma there is loss, and where there is loss there is a necessary grieving process to come to a place of acceptance. Whether your touchstone memory involves actual losses or separations, or emotional abuse or neglect, sexual abuse, domestic violence, or physical abuse (i.e., common traumas associated with adult depression), the shared reality across these experiences is that inherent needs for the innocent child who lives on in you were either lost or never met. That is, your normal and natural needs for safety, protection, love, and compassion—exhibited through a caregiver's attunement, attention, appreciation, affection, and acceptance—were insufficiently fulfilled or even violated.

It is vital for your healing to identify what needs were not met to help you grieve healthily and learn to self-fulfill those unmet needs through this process and beyond. Accordingly, you may find it beneficial during the reprocessing sessions to 1) ensure that you are grieving by fully acknowledging your pain without trying to control it, and 2) start to help meet the unmet needs of the still-wounded child that lives within you. Draw upon the attachment figure resource you built in chapter 1 and continue to integrate the mindfulness and self-compassion skills from chapter 3—these skills will help you be more lovingly present with your experience during this process. For instance, during the reprocessing sets you might draw from RAIN to help you *recognize, allow,* and attune to the pain the child in you is feeling as you *investigate* your younger self's internal experiences, to then offer the applicable acknowledgment, compassion, *nurturance,* or protection.

As part of being a human with defense mechanisms, you may notice yourself focusing on blaming your caregiver or other people involved, which is a normal part of the process. However, as blaming to excess is often a sneaky form of denial, make sure that you shift your attention inward so you are tending to your emotions beneath the blaming—hurt, grief, anger, shock, sadness, shame, fear, etc.—to productively facilitate your process of acceptance. While it is true that what happened to you is not your fault, it is also true that you are the sole person responsible for your healing. *You are the one with the choice to let go.* Remember to practice being patient with yourself on this challenging journey. Let go of any expectations you might be holding with regard to timelines so that you're not taken away from the present moment—where you need to be in order to know and accept what you're feeling. When you are able to recognize and label the grief-stricken emotions during your sets of fast bilateral stimulation, also make sure to locate and attune to where you feel those emotions in your body and practice genuinely telling yourself *it's okay.*

On the other extreme, also beware of any tendency to overly extend compassion to the caregiver or other person's behavior as a sneaky way of denying your own pain by minimizing or dismissing the emotional impact of their behavior on you. Ideally, there is compassion for both yourself and others. This might look like a balance between saying yes, the hurtful caregiver probably did not intend to cause harm and had their own unresolved trauma, *and* the outcome or reality is that you feel valid emotional pain that EMDR is helping you to accept and integrate as you move forward. It is valid to acknowledge that the touchstone memory that may have involved the hurtful caregiver—along with other connected subsequent memories—understandably triggered a felt sense of yourself as defective, unacceptable, and unworthy of love and respect.

Remember that your emotions are essential teachers that, when attuned to, help you strengthen your sense of self. A common outcome of being emotionally neglected, ironically, is learning to neglect and otherwise not acknowledge your own emotions. A further irony, and where you start to recognize intergenerational trauma, is that your emotionally neglectful or abusive caregiver was probably repeating patterns *they* learned from their upbringing, and so on and so forth—which is why you may have deduced that they possibly did not intend to cause harm. This does not *ever* make neglectful or abusive behavior acceptable, but it does provide a realistic and balanced understanding as to *why* it occurred to help you not personalize it by believing it was your fault or that you deserved it. That understanding of others' unconscious projections will generate further compassion and healing, knowing that the depression you're carrying is actually not just your own. It also helps you come to terms with the reality that your relationship to your caregiver or other person who caused you harm is not black or white, as you probably also have experienced positive memories of and feelings for them. It is vital that you sort through all of these gray areas to make sure you are validating the full range of your experiences and associated emotions, as to avoid this would be to remain in denial.

With the mindfulness and self-compassion skills you have been starting to build upon in this process, you may find an inclination to learn to acknowledge and care for yourself by applying these skills to heal the grieving child within you. This application can happen both within the reprocessing sessions and outside of them if you notice becoming triggered. Again, you may find it especially helpful to draw upon the RAIN acronym from chapter 3 in this application. The intention here is to go back and ultimately *fulfill the unmet needs you have identified from this and associated memories that are contributing to your depression.* That way, the deliberate going back into the past is productive, providing a space for you to essentially reparent yourself in the protective, compassionate, loving, and emotionally attuned ways that you needed. That is how you find your wholeness and power within.

CHAPTER 7

Reprocessing and Closure Phases (5–7): **Transforming Your Relationship Within**

Your task is not to seek for love, but merely to seek and find all the barriers within yourself that you have built against it.

—Rumi

If you have returned to the target memory and your SUD is a 0 out of 10, as in you have reprocessed it over the course of at least several sessions and it feels neutral both in your head and body, congratulations—this is a major feat! Take a few moments to notice how you feel now compared to when you first started reprocessing the target memory at the beginning of the desensitization phase. Recognize and appreciate that this is a result of your courageous efforts, and continue to engage in self-compassion. Your genuine efforts are always worthy of recognition and praise.

You are now ready to proceed to the installation phase (5). This transition from phase 4 to phase 5 can happen within the same session or alternatively be started up as a new session, depending on when within the session you completed phase 4. This chapter also includes phases 6 and 7 which are comprised of a body scan and instructions for closing out each session, respectively.

Phase Five: Installation

The intention of the installation phase is to help you reassociate the target memory with a positive belief (identified during phase 3), and to strengthen the validity of that belief. It is still considered a reprocessing phase and has the goal of *trait change* (a long-lasting change in perspective or attitude, versus *state change*, a more temporary shift in emotion like with the resourcing exercises you did in phase 2), meaning you will continue doing longer sets of fast bilateral stimulation like you did in the prior desensitization phase—between twenty to forty sets and as fast as you can tolerate. However, it is unlikely to take as much time to complete compared to phase 4, since now there is minimal negative emotional charge associated with the target memory.

This does not mean that this phase is any less important. Being able to strengthen positive feelings and beliefs is crucial for transcending your depression and improving your overall quality of life. Remember, the goal of EMDR therapy is not only about reducing your depression by fostering acceptance, but increasing a positive and secure sense of yourself. So not only do you want to look back at the hardships you faced with the absence of shame, guilt, or fear, you also want to look back with feelings of compassion, appreciation, and resilience for making it through those hardships. Phase 5 focuses on this latter component to help you come into your highest authentic expression of self.

Identify Your Positive Cognition

Refer back to the positive cognition you wrote down during phase 3 (chapter 6). Assess if this positive belief still aligns with the target memory. When you bring up the memory, do these words still fit? Or is there another positive statement that fits even better?

As a reminder, there are no right or wrong answers here. We ask these questions because sometimes the positive cognition holds true, whereas other times the desensitization phase takes us down a road we hadn't imagined, requiring a different positive cognition. Sometimes the initial statement is too broad and needs to be specified for the target memory to be more realistic and aligned. For instance, perhaps the initial positive cognition you wrote was about the situation not being your fault, and you want to extend this statement to include something about being a strong or good person. Use this as an opportunity to go inward and trust your instinctive response based on the process you went through during phase 4 and how it led to a place of neutrality. That is, when you recall this memory without feeling the emotional charge and sensitivity you once did, what have you learned? With that clearer perspective, what does the memory say about you as a person now? *Choose a statement that is the most meaningful to you.* Listen to and trust the cues from your body.

Once you have clarified your positive cognition, write it down. Now, bring up the memory and your positive cognition together in your mind as you reassess the *validity of this cognition.* As you bring up the target memory and this positive statement, on a scale from 1–7, where 1 feels completely false and 7 feels completely true, how true does this statement feel to you *now?* Write down your current validity number. The number you identify now will typically be higher than it was during phase 3.

Integrate Your Positive Cognition

Hold the memory and the words of your positive cognition together as you start a sequence of twenty to forty sets of fast bilateral stimulation. *Take a breath, let it go. What are you noticing now?* Once you have expressed or recorded your experience, whatever it may be, *go with that* as you start a subsequent sequence of fast bilateral stimulation for twenty to forty sets, adjusting the number of sets based on your individual response. *Take a breath, let it go. What are you noticing now?* As long as you continue to notice changes from sequence to sequence, express or record what you're noticing each time and *go with that* as you start another twenty to forty sets of bilateral stimulation.

Much like you found during phase 4, phase 5 does not have a predictable course. Thus, you are again being challenged to trust your brain's natural ability to heal itself in the particular manner that it needs to. If the current validity of your cognition is closer to a 6 or 7 on the scale, you will likely notice a strengthening of the positive cognition and associated feelings as you do the fast sets of bilateral stimulation.

You might also notice connections to possible memories or situations that block it from being a solid 7 during the bilateral stimulation. If that happens, your brain is still in the process of clearing out connected memories; simply allow yourself to go down these necessary detours without feeling pressure to go back to the positive statement and target memory. If you get to a point where you are no longer noticing changes from sequence to sequence, then bring yourself back to the target memory and the words of your updated positive cognition to reassess the validity of the cognition.

- **If you recorded a 6:** If after going through multiple sequences of twenty to forty sets of fast bilateral stimulation you noticed a strengthening of positive feelings and experiences, go back to the target memory and reassess the validity of your cognition. From 1–7, where 1 feels completely false and 7 feels completely true, how true does the memory feel to you now? *Go with that* and reengage in the sequence of twenty to forty sets of fast bilateral stimulation. *Take a breath, let it go,* process your experience, and repeat this entire sequence until the positive feelings are no longer getting any stronger. Once the validity of the cognition feels like a solid 7, do one sequence of twenty to forty sets of fast bilateral stimulation, then proceed to phase 6.

- **If you recorded lower than a 6:** It is possible that either the positive cognition needs some revision or there are residual disturbances blocking it from feeling completely true that need to be reprocessed. Again, trust that your brain will make connections to any residual disturbances that need to be reprocessed, and as per usual, use any disturbances that come up as opportunities to be lovingly present with your experience. If you need any probing, consider this: *what prevents the number from being a 7?* Whatever comes to mind... *go with that* as you restart twenty to forty sets of fast bilateral stimulation. Try not to put a timeline on how long this process is going to take so you can practice unconditional love and acceptance. Allow your thoughts, feelings, and memories to go on their necessary trajectories to help you find resolution, and trust that that is exactly what they are doing. As a reminder, there are no rights or wrongs, and you are being challenged to trust yourself.

Sometimes the validity of the positive cognition progressing above a 5 or 6 is prevented by a dysfunctional blocking belief from a *feeder memory* that needs processing. If this happens to you, put the current memory reprocessing on pause, then target the feeder memory with a full course of EMDR (phases 3–8). This is necessary in order to complete phase 5 for the original target memory. The direct questioning, floatback, and affect scan techniques from phase 1 are intended to pinpoint the most representative and earliest memory to prevent this from occurring; however, with complex trauma and their associated defense mechanisms sometimes these feeder memories do not pop up until later in the process. Trust that this is a part of your personal process and that you didn't do anything wrong if you find yourself in this position. You must learn to believe in yourself unconditionally!

If you are still actively working on the installation phase but need to pause before reaching a validity score of 7, follow the instructions below for phase 7 (closure). These techniques—debriefing, containment, and resourcing—allow you to pause the installation phase until you are ready to return. Then, when you resume your next EMDR session, you will revisit the installation phase by reassessing the validity of your positive cognition (on a scale from 1–7) as you bring up your touchstone memory. Using the instructions at the beginning of this section, hold the memory and the positive cognition in your mind while doing twenty to forty sets of fast bilateral stimulation. Continue to *take a breath, let it go,* and check in. As long as you notice changes from sequence to sequence, *go with that,* continuing to do sets of bilateral stimulation. Once the validity feels like a solid 7, continue on to phase 6.

A final thought about phase 5 regarding the validity of the positive cognition: in some cases, people find that a 6 is as high and solid as the validity number is going to get for them. EMDR considers the validity of the cognition in these cases to be *ecologically valid*, that is, that the treatment effectively transfers to real life. If this is the case for you and you feel confident in this assertion, then congratulations! Notice your feelings of confidence and assuredness about this number seeming to be the most appropriate given the context, and proceed to phase 6.

Phase Six: Body Scan

Once you've reached a 7 (or an ecologically valid 6) for your target memory, you're ready to complete a body scan. Doing a body scan is a way to ensure this positive cognition is ingrained in your mind, body, and spirit. As you might recall from chapter 2, maladaptively stored memories affect not only beliefs and emotions, but also physical sensations. Phase 6 intends to directly target any discernible physical symptoms associated with the target memory. These sensations may disappear on their own within several sets without making any other associations. Sometimes, however, focusing on the core of these sensations will open up other channels, bringing up memories that need their own full course of EMDR treatment (phases 3–8). The body scan is still considered a reprocessing phase and has the goal of trait change, meaning that you will continue doing longer sets of fast bilateral stimulation like you did in the prior two reprocessing phases.

Body Scan Steps

Go ahead and close your eyes. Bring up the original memory as you experience it *now* and the words of your positive cognition. Then, bring your attention to the different parts of your body, starting with your head and working your way downward. Notice and stop if you find an area that holds any tension, tightness, or otherwise unusual sensation. If you identify such an area, open your eyes and focus your attention with curiosity on the core of those sensations as you start twenty to forty sets of fast bilateral stimulation. Continue sets of fast bilateral stimulation until the sensations subside.

Then go back to closing your eyes and recall the memory and positive cognition while you complete another body scan from head to toe. If you again notice any tension, tightness, or unusual sensation, open your eyes to apply bilateral stimulation until the sensations subside. Continue repeating this process until you notice a complete clearance or that it otherwise seems *ecologically adaptive* (i.e., if you have chronic pain or an acute injury where it wouldn't make sense for a particular sensation to fully disappear).

The body scan phase is considered complete when you can hold in mind the original memory along with your positive cognition without finding residual disturbance in your body. If you notice, alternatively, any positive or pleasant sensations in your body during the scan, you can apply bilateral stimulation to strengthen those sensations.

Phase Seven: Closure

Although some touchstone or target memories can be sufficiently processed within a single session, this is not typically the case. See the table for the differences in resolved and unresolved target memories as defined by EMDR. Regardless of which of the active reprocessing phases you are in toward the end of a given session, each session should reserve some time at the end to appropriately close the session. You want to be transitioning out of your sessions in a relatively clear and neutral state of mind so that you can effectively contain the disturbing material and engage in your life the way you intend to for the long run.

Unresolved Memory	Resolved Memory
Still feel disturbance in the body *in this current moment* when thinking about the memory	No disturbance is felt in the body *in this current moment* when thinking about the memory
The SUD is greater than a 0	The SUD is a 0

Unresolved Memory	Resolved Memory
The validity of the positive cognition is less than 7	The validity of the positive cognition is a 7 (or ecologically valid 6)
The body scan is not clear	The body scan is clear

The active reprocessing phases, especially the desensitization phase, can be particularly emotionally, physically, and mentally heavy and draining. Being in a state of depression can already contribute to these kinds of feelings, which is why it is recommended that you 1) limit your reprocessing sessions to no more than sixty minutes and 2) leave ample time at the end to close up and transition out of the session—aiming for between five to fifteen minutes depending on what phase you are in and how activated your system is. Remember, slow and steady progress is both more realistic and better for the long term. Even though EMDR therapy is often a chosen modality because it does produce rapid insights and results, there is no way to rush through the process of healing. Part of practicing self-compassion is slowing down, giving yourself grace, and learning to be patient with yourself and your journey so that you're faithfully going through the flow of life versus trying to control it because you don't like it.

Regardless of whether your target memory is completely or incompletely processed, make sure that during the days in between your EMDR sessions with your therapist that you are containing dysfunctional material and engaging in your life in ways that are nourishing. Recall from chapter 4 that your life itself can be considered therapy, so plan accordingly to maximize your time. Part of building greater self-compassion is creating a daily routine comprised of activities that both make you feel genuinely happy and are congruent with your true sense of self. Remember, you *deserve* to feel happy and at home with yourself—and you have the strength and power within you to make this your reality. Start to treat yourself in the way you deserve with regard to every daily activity you choose to engage in so you can continue to increase the experience of pleasure, joy, love, and authenticity.

Closure for Incomplete Target Memory Sessions

On the subject of practicing self-compassion, start each closure phase you encounter with a check-in of how you are feeling physically, emotionally, and mentally. Take the opportunity to express sincere appreciation for your efforts to reinforce that you are giving space and attention to your inner world in the most loving way that you can. Practice offering yourself genuine words of encouragement, validation, and compassion. For instance, try saying to yourself: *That was incredibly heavy and hard today. You did such a great job trusting yourself with the process and allowing yourself to tend to some deep pain.* You might practice this while at the same time offering yourself soothing self-touch like placing your hands over your heart, holding your hands together and rubbing the sides of them with your thumbs, or giving yourself a hug and rubbing your arms with your opposite hands to show affection.

Depending on the level of emotional and physical activation within your system, you may need a containment exercise. If you notice feeling anxious and distressed toward the ending of a session, use this observation as an indication to bring up your imaginary container from phase 2 (chapter 5), remembering to close your eyes and take several slow, deep breaths as you picture your container and allow any disturbing thoughts, feelings, and memories to be sealed into your container. Give yourself as much time as you need for this exercise, and be sure that you finish by sealing up your container in the way your imagination wants. Then, open your eyes and notice any shifts in your mind, body, and spirit with this.

To further shift your energetic state away from anxiety and distress, consider bringing up the cue word or phrase from your safe/calm state that you completed during phase 2 (chapter 5). Again, close your eyes, picturing your safe/calm state and the cue word or phrase you associated with it. Notice any shifts in your body as you do this. During this process, you may also find that new images that bring feelings of safety and calm spontaneously arise—if so, congratulate yourself, and welcome more of these experiences! This shows that you are expanding your repertoire of safe and pleasant internal states to access, which speaks to you building further strength and resilience. The more memories and experiences you can draw upon that are associated with feelings of safety and calm, the merrier.

To enhance any calm or other pleasant sensations elicited from the safe/calm state exercise, do four to eight sets of *slow* bilateral stimulation. Continue several sequences of four to eight sets of slow bilateral stimulation as long as the pleasant feelings strengthen. Give yourself permission to feel calm and relaxed—and also give yourself grace for feeling tired from the heavy reprocessing session you just completed. You may need to remind yourself that this is to be expected in the aftermath of heavy reprocessing.

Again, offer yourself praise and validation for your efforts in shifting your internal state as needed. Then, once you've established moving into this more stabilized and neutral state, give yourself some space to reflect on and debrief the session you just completed. As you consider your experience, what positive summary can you make that expresses either how you feel or what you have learned or gained? A lot of processing and learning happens during each session, so the answers here can vary. As a reminder, there are no right or wrong answers. See this as an opportunity to continue practicing trusting your instincts on what has been most impactful during your latest reprocessing session. Write down this summary in your journal or notebook.

Lastly, it is important to manage your expectations regarding the aftermath of your reprocessing sessions. Anticipate possible residual disturbances that may come up in between any incomplete target memory sessions. That is, the processing from your session may continue over the course of the next few days, although this is not always the case. If the dysfunctional material has not yet been fully processed, though, there is a greater likelihood that your system will continue the processing between sessions at a higher level of disturbance despite the containment and relaxation exercises you used to close the session. Follow the same directions that you did during the reprocessing sets—let whatever happens happen and simply observe your experience without judging it. Continue to draw upon your container, safe place, and other internal resources you've built to help bring you back to center; don't feel like you need to "solve" anything in between sessions. To reduce that disturbance indefinitely, remind yourself that the target memory will continue to be processed at the next session.

Nevertheless, in between sessions, it is important that you monitor and record any sort of disturbance that arises using your journal or notebook. This record should include any memories, dreams, thoughts, and situations that are in any way disturbing to you. Keeping such a log will allow you to be able to remember anything of relevance to share with your therapist. It will also allow you to continue increasing in self-awareness of your triggers and any patterns that may inform targets for future EMDR sessions. Of course, make sure that you not only write down anything that you notice coming up, but use relaxation techniques like your containment exercise and your safe place to help reduce distress. Consider other self-soothing strategies as well like going for a walk outside, snuggling with your pet, listening to music, drawing, knitting, taking a bath, watching an uplifting or funny movie or TV show, or a combination of these.

The TICES Log

The TICES log, which stands for Trigger, Image, Cognition, Emotion, and Sensations/SUD, is a guide to help you record your in-between session experiences—this includes not only disturbing events but also any pleasant ones which can help provide balance. You do not need to go into detail with each of the columns as this is a log to help remind you of possible targets for future sessions. Note that for each triggering experience you have, you may not fill out every single one of the six columns after the date column. For instance, sometimes disturbing images and memories emerge whereas at other times you may notice only disturbing emotions and sensations. Try your best to break down the disturbance into each of these parts, and then engage in a relaxation exercise as much as needed to take care of your mind, body, and spirit. A blank TICES log is also available on the free tools site for this book at http://www.newharbinger.com/56975.

Date	Trigger	Image	Cognition	Emotion	Sensations/ SUD
	Learning about a friend getting engaged		I'm a failure, I'm unworthy of love	Shame, sadness, fear	Pit in stomach, chest tight and heavy
	Partner's mood appears off	Flashes of when my mom was upset with me as a child	I did something wrong, I'm bad	Anger, fear, guilt	Heart palpitations, chest tight
	Dream about being back at childhood home	The family room		Sadness, helplessness, grief	Heaviness in chest
	Partner's hug			Love, relief	Warmth in heart/chest, heavy but light feelings

Your awareness of any disturbing experiences in between sessions is a sign of growth. Therefore, even if it feels uncomfortable, try to recognize and remind yourself that this is a good thing. Congratulate yourself for noticing and recording such experiences. Sometimes when you bring up deeply buried painful experiences you went through, you may notice feeling initially worse before you start to feel better. This is completely normal to experience!

There is no growth without pain and discomfort, and it is important to repeatedly remind yourself that this is a part of the processing. There is no way around it; you must go through it, and the good news about this is that you're allowed to do so at a pace that works for you. Do not feel like you need to solve these experiences on your own, and remember to use your container and other self-soothing strategies—you are allowed to keep these things stored in your container until your next therapy session so that you can continue to engage in a meaningful life. You might benefit from creating encouraging sticky-note reminders to post around areas you visit on a daily basis like your desk, workstation, mirror, bedside, bathroom, and kitchen. Here are some examples:

- *This is old stuff coming up—you're safe now.*
- *You've got this!*
- *I believe in you!*
- *I'm so proud of you!*
- *I'm so glad you're here.*
- *You're doing amazing work.*
- *Your efforts are worthy of praise.*
- *Everything is working out for your highest good.*
- *Out of this experience good will come.*
- *It's okay to not be okay.*
- *It's okay to feel sad and scared.*
- *I've got your back, always.*
- *We're gonna get through this together, always!*
- *I'm here for you always.*
- *I love you no matter what!*

Closure for Completed Target Memory Sessions

If you have achieved resolution and made it through the end of the body scan phase, congratulations! This is a huge feat that absolutely deserves your acknowledgment, praise, and celebration. Start this celebration by validating and appreciating all the excellent work you have put in to get here. How are you feeling? Give yourself permission to feel whatever you feel here and record this experience in your journal or notebook.

Typically at this stage there is not any need for safety or stabilization with containment or safe state exercises since the completion of the body scan phase suggests there is full clearance, neutrality, and maybe even positive emotions and sensations. Instead, continue journaling: record what has been most useful, or what you have learned or gained, from this latest session.

Continue to manage expectations when it comes to experiences in between EMDR therapy sessions. The processing may continue after this latest session—you may or may not notice new insights, thoughts, memories, physical sensations, or dreams. Make sure to continue to record anything that you notice that comes up, and draw upon your container, safe state exercise, and other coping skills as needed. You may continue to use the TICES log to help organize how you record such experiences. Remember to practice appreciating the full range of triggering experiences so you can recognize that this is part of being fully alive!

Lastly, if you have made it this far, a celebration beyond the initial encouraging and validating words is definitely in order! Remember that this is also what self-compassion is all about. How do you treat your loved ones when they have accomplished something, whether big or small? With this evolving and increasingly self-compassionate version of yourself you're actively creating, how are you going to treat yourself in the manner that you deserve? Make sure you take the space to celebrate in ways that are congruent with your long-term goals and nourishing for you personally. Trust yourself, and have fun!

CHAPTER 8

Reevaluation Phase (8): Ongoing Self-Reflections

The basic principle of spiritual life is that our problems become the very place to discover wisdom and love.

—Jack Kornfield

Regardless of which of the reprocessing phases (4–6) you may be in the middle of completing, the reevaluation phase takes place at the beginning of *each* EMDR therapy session once the reprocessing of the touchstone memory has begun. Broadly, *reevaluation* aims to understand how EMDR is progressing in keeping you on track with your goals. This phase was briefly covered during chapter 6 and will be covered in comprehensive detail in the present chapter. When you have gotten to this phase of treatment it is because you have at least started phase 4—desensitization of the touchstone memory you selected during phase 1. Phase 8 will help you best determine your next immediate steps for the session and long-term steps for your overall treatment plan. You are making significant progress as you venture through the middle of some seriously painful but meaningful inner work—congratulations!

Reevaluation has its own phase due to the crucial aspect of appropriate follow-ups once reprocessing of a memory has begun. As a whole, phase 8 considers these four overlapping factors:

1. Whether the current touchstone memory being targeted has been resolved and integrated;

2. Whether associated material has been triggered that needs to be addressed;

3. Whether all identified targets of your depression have been reprocessed—such that you feel at peace with your past, empowered in your present, and relatively confident in making more desirable choices for your future; and

4. Whether you have satisfactorily integrated your evolved and ever-evolving self within your own healthy social system.

These overlapping factors are essential to the success of EMDR therapy and will be discussed throughout this chapter; they are reflected in EMDR's standard three-pronged protocol, which targets dysfunctional material from the past and present and then focuses on adaptive changes for the future.

Successful outcomes in EMDR therapy require the appropriate utilization of all three prongs—past, present, and future. Once the dysfunctional material from childhood memories has been sufficiently processed, each connected present trigger and related future situation (identified in phase 1) is addressed through reprocessing and integrating a positive *future template*, a technique focused on a desired response in a future situation. For instance, during the assessment phase of treatment, you looked at present-day triggering situations to better understand what dysfunctional material from your past was being triggered. Currently, you are in the middle of addressing the dysfunctionally stored childhood memories in which your present-day experiences of depression are rooted. Once these are sufficiently processed, you will go back to assessing your present-day triggers to process any remaining disturbance and feel better equipped to handle similar future situations.

This chapter is divided into the following sections that depict the different trajectories of phase 8, depending on whether your last session ended with an unresolved or a resolved target memory and whether you've processed all targets from the past that are influencing the present:

1. Starting a session following a reprocessing session

2. The potential for processing new material

3. Resuming reprocessing phases for an incomplete target memory

4. Choosing next targets once a memory is complete

5. Incorporating a future template

Starting a Session Following a Reprocessing Session

Reprocessing dysfunctionally stored material can have a rapid and profound impact on your thoughts, feelings, and behaviors. Even one reprocessing session can change how you relate to others, which in turn can bring up both new and old issues to incorporate into your EMDR treatment. At the beginning of every session during phase 8, you'll check in on how effective EMDR has been so far, how well your touchstone memory has been resolved, and if there are any earlier memories coming into your conscious awareness that need to be processed. When starting a new processing session, you'll first reflect on the following questions with your therapist:

- Related to the primary issue or issues you identified during phase 1 (covered in chapter 4) that you have started working on, what have you noticed that is new or different in your life since your last session?

- Have you noticed any changes in your thoughts, feelings, dreams, or behavior?

- Has anyone in your life pointed out any changes?

- Do you have any new memories or insights as you think about these issues today?

Give yourself some time and space to reflect on your answers to each of the above questions. It is essential to recognize each and every change you can remember that you have made along the way, no matter how big or small you judge them to be. Each one counts, and the reflection itself provides an opportunity for you to continue building a more compassionate relationship with yourself.

Recall the TICES log you were provided with from the closure phase (7), covered in chapter 7, and the overall emphasis that was made on recording any sorts of relevant experiences that come up in between therapy sessions. Sometimes people notice feeling worse, sometimes better, and sometimes a combination of feeling worse in some respects and better in others. The risks of EMDR therapy are essentially the same as its benefits—you're going to *feel* things! To feel, especially if you've become good at habitually numbing and blocking your feelings, is a major sign of growth. This is true *even* if the feelings are painful and uncomfortable. Unlocking deeply buried painful feelings is going to also maximize your experiences of joy and love, so try to remind yourself why you're doing this. You are worth it!

Any changes that you noticed coming up are a sign that your system is processing dysfunctional material. Either way, you are making progress and this is fantastic. Reflect upon how you managed any disturbances that arose. What new and healthy coping skills did you draw upon that are worthy of your recognition and praise? What former unhealthy coping skills did you notice being able to steer away from more so than in the past? How are the practices of mindfulness and self-compassion toward your internal landscape coming along?

Pull out your TICES log from your journal for a more specific review and prioritization of your most triggering experiences since the last session. In what context did you feel worse or better? Did you see any of the triggering experiences coming up as being connected to the ongoing reprocessing you've started with the touchstone memory? Did other childhood memories come to the surface, or do you need some help from your therapist recognizing what your most recent triggers are connected to? Discuss all of these with your therapist, especially those that you feel need further understanding or resolution, as they might inform possible targets for your EMDR therapy.

For the most recent triggering experiences that need further processing, you may consider drawing upon the direct questioning, floatback, and affect scan techniques introduced during the initial assessment phase (1) in chapter 4. These might take you back to the touchstone memory itself or to memories that are connected to the touchstone memory—assuming that the negative cognitions are the same. Alternatively, and depending on what is happening in your life, it is possible that the most recent triggering experience or experiences are related to a *different* (but interconnected) wound and associated root memory than the one you have started to target.

Anticipating the Potential for New Processing

Why might there be a necessity for new processing while you're already in the middle of reprocessing phases for a touchstone memory? For one, a rapidly effective therapy like EMDR that helps you change your internal landscape will in turn affect how you see and relate to your external world, including and especially in your interactions with others across different types of settings. The reprocessing phases (4–6) can shed light on patterns you hadn't noticed before, leading to new insights that you might become more aware of across work, home, or social environments.

The increased feelings of self-efficacy that often result from reprocessing sessions can empower you to interact with others in different ways. You might begin to change the way you respond to situations, relating differently than your previously ingrained patterns. Or, if you notice that you are already relating to others differently, you may feel some doubt or anxiety as you're stepping into less-than-familiar territory. As such, it may be important to put the resuming of reprocessing the touchstone memory on a temporary hold to attend to any acute interpersonal or social issues that come up during the process. However, the typical rule of thumb is that the dysfunctional material from the touchstone memory should be processed *before* moving on to another target (unless there's a feeder memory)—and any acute issues coming up may just be a continuation of processing old stuff. Nonetheless, new disturbances that arise might need to be added as future targets in your treatment plan. This will be best determined in collaboration with your EMDR therapist and as you continue the reprocessing. Remember to trust your unfolding process!

Another common reason that new processing might be required is that the combination of your increasing self-awareness, courage, and reprocessing of the touchstone memory may uncover repressed memories connected to the touchstone memory. When you start to face the fears associated with buried memories of your past repeatedly, over time you will notice an increased strength and resilience. Often as a result of getting past one fear, other greater fears—like even more deeply buried memories—will present themselves. If this happens, congratulate yourself; recognize this experience as a sign that you are actually growing in mental and emotional strength, even and especially if it doesn't necessarily feel like you are. Other dysfunctional material arising during the process is *absolutely not* a sign of failure and instead speaks to a natural unfolding process of you unearthing higher levels of conscious awareness.

If the repressed memory that surfaced during the reprocessing of the current touchstone memory happened chronologically earlier in your childhood, then you may need to target this *feeder memory*—especially if the associated negative cognition and emotions are the same. Doing this will allow for more sufficient processing, meaning that when you return to your original touchstone memory, it is likely to have become resolved because it's actually rooted in this earlier memory. The techniques used during the assessment phase are intended to try to prevent this from happening by getting to the root memories tied to your depression; however, because of the nature of the unconscious and how ingrained defense mechanisms can work to keep things hidden, earlier repressed memories can resurface while you're in the midst of reprocessing what you thought were the earliest roots. If this happens, it is okay! Remember that the growth journey is not linear; it is often filled with necessary detours. The most helpful attitude to adopt is one where you believe and appreciate that each and every part of the journey is happening for your highest good and evolution.

If new processing of earlier roots needs to be addressed, put the current touchstone memory on hold. Identify the earlier root memory as the updated touchstone memory to target, and apply standard procedures for phases 3–6 of EMDR—remembering to close each session and open up each subsequent session using procedures for phases 7 and 8.

You would then return to the original touchstone memory to reevaluate whether it has been sufficiently processed (i.e., with a SUD of zero, a VOC of greater than 6, and a clear body scan) or not (i.e., a SUD of greater than zero, a VOC of less than 7, or uncleared body scan), and then proceed accordingly.

Resuming Reprocessing Phases for an Incomplete Target Memory

If it is clear to you that any recent triggering experiences you've had since your last reprocessing session are connected to your touchstone memory and merely a sign that your system is continuing to digest the dysfunctionally stored material, then you will pick back up on reprocessing that memory and continue doing so until it is sufficiently processed. Or, if you've taken a necessary detour and discover an updated touchstone memory, you will target that memory. Remember that a dysfunctionally stored memory is considered sufficiently processed when the SUD is 0, leading you to complete the installation phase until the validity of your positive cognition is 7, followed by a clear body scan. With continued reprocessing of a disturbing memory, you will typically notice that the vividness of the image associated with the worst part of the memory will dissipate, as will any associated emotional charge and physical symptoms. However, sometimes the vividness and SUD can go up depending on various factors, so it is important to continue to practice not judging your experience.

Have your environment prepared to be as comfortable as you can and restart the bilateral stimulation. The following steps are the procedures to resume the desensitization phase (4) for an incomplete target memory:

1. Bring up the memory you have been working on. What is the image that represents the worst part of it now? (Sometimes the worst part shifts, sometimes it doesn't. Remember, there is no right or wrong in this process. Simply notice what comes up and trust yourself!).

2. What emotions are you experiencing now? On a scale from 0–10, where 0 is neutral or no disturbance and 10 is the highest disturbance you can imagine, how disturbing does the memory feel to you *now*?

3. Where do you feel it in your body?

4. Now, bring up the experience, notice the emotions and sensations you're having, and *let it go wherever it needs to go* as you start a cycle of twenty to forty sets of fast bilateral stimulation.

5. *Let it go, take a breath.* What are you noticing now? Express or record what you noticed, and then *go with that* as you start another sequence of twenty to forty sets of fast bilateral stimulation. As long as you continue to notice changes from sequence to sequence, *go with that* as you continue the sequence of twenty to forty sets of fast bilateral stimulation.

If you experience no changes in two consecutive sequences, go back to reassess your current experience of the touchstone memory. *When you bring up the memory as you experience it now, what are you noticing now?* Express or record your experience, and then simply *go with that* as you start twenty to forty sets of fast bilateral stimulation, allowing whatever needs to happen to happen as your brain and body process the experience in the way that they need to. *Take a breath, let it go. What are you noticing now?* Continue to repeat this sequence—twenty to forty sets of fast bilateral stimulation, pause to notice, express, and record your experience, and *go with that*—as long as new information is experienced. Remember you're safe here now as you're looking back, and that this is just old stuff that needs to come up to be acknowledged by your loving and curious presence so you can keep moving forward.

If you do not experience any changes across two consecutive sequences, return to the touchstone memory to reassess your SUD level. When you bring up the memory as you experience it now, on a scale of 0 to 10, where 0 is neutral or no disturbance and 10 is the highest disturbance you can imagine, how disturbing does the memory feel to you now?

- If your SUD is greater than 2, *go with that* as you start fast bilateral stimulation for twenty to forty sets.

- If your SUD is 1 or 2, *where do you feel that in your body?* Go *with that* as you start fast bilateral stimulation for twenty to forty sets. In either situation above, go back to repeating the usual sequence as long as new information is being produced with each set.

- If your SUD is 0, *go with that* as you start at least one sequence of twenty to forty sets of bilateral stimulation. *What are you noticing now?* As long as it remains neutral or you are not noticing changes, you are ready to proceed to phase 5.

Remember that it typically takes several EMDR therapy sessions to complete the reprocessing phases for a single touchstone memory. Try to notice and let go of any negative judgments or comparisons about where you are in your process that might come up in your mind, drawing upon the clouds in the sky metaphor from chapter 4 as needed. Recognize that the intentions of such judgments or comparisons are likely to help you move forward, and that these are old patterns from your depression that you're working to change, so that you're treating yourself with greater compassion instead of the criticism that fuels your depression. You might practice repeating the following more positive, compassionate, and realistic affirmations:

- *Matters of the heart take time to heal.*

- *Reversing ingrained patterns of thinking, feeling, and relating to my thoughts and feelings takes time.*

- *I'm worthy of the time and effort it takes to change my ingrained unhelpful patterns.*

These statements can help you learn to be more patient with yourself when you notice bouts of self-criticism coming up. Try to be fully honest with yourself about what you're noticing and how you feel without trying to rush your healing and overcoming of your past. Remember that practicing nonjudgment of your experience and trusting your unique process are key here. There are no rights or wrongs. You're doing great!

Do not try to rush to the finish line, which will backfire on your need to reverse unhealthy defense mechanisms that keep you from truly accepting your experience. The goal is acceptance—not to control and get rid of your experience, which is the opposite. The more present and engaged you are with your journey with an attitude of compassionate curiosity, the more you transform your experience in the way that you're truly asking for in the big picture. Once you have reached resolution of your touchstone memory (i.e., a SUD of zero, a VOC of greater than 7, and a clear body scan), congratulations! You are now ready to revisit your overall treatment plan to determine next possible targets for EMDR therapy.

Reviewing Your Treatment Plan: Choosing Next Targets

The intention of the first prong of the EMDR therapy protocol is to resolve the dysfunctional material of the past so that you can be freed to live more in the present. The second prong then aims to understand what current people and situations in your life elicit the unhelpful reactions driven by that dysfunctional past material. Typically, the resolution of the target memory in turn leads to less disturbing associated early memories and present-day situations—especially the initial triggers you identified during the assessment phase (1) in chapter 4. The changes in the present therefore tend to automatically happen without directly targeting the present-day situations.

Once you have sufficiently processed your first touchstone memory, take a moment to check back with the initial present-day triggers associated with your primary presenting issue that you identified during phase 1 in chapter 4. Are they all now neutral? *For any initial triggers that are still disturbing and did not become neutral, apply standard procedures for phases 3–6 prior to starting phases 3–6 for a new touchstone memory.*

As described in the above sections, sometimes new situations and triggers will arise in between sessions. The emergence of new triggers can lead to identifying a new touchstone memory. If you have achieved resolution of one touchstone memory thus far in your journey, then it is likely that there are other touchstone memories to target—people often target a total of about ten disturbing childhood memories, meaning that they will cycle through a full EMDR protocol *at least* ten times. Therefore, *you should prioritize continuing to resolve those touchstone memories.*

Again, any new triggers that arose during phases 4–6 of your now resolved touchstone memory should be considered a natural unfolding of your process that can help identify subsequent touchstone memories to target in your overall treatment plan. That is, continue to practice trusting that your brain knows how it needs to heal itself to fully recover from each of the unresolved wounds of the past that contribute to your current depression. Remind your depression-prone mind that everything is working out for your highest good and unfolding as it needs to for the evolution of your highest consciousness. Use your personal affirmations discussed in the last chapter as needed!

Just as you did during the assessment phase, during the reevaluation phase you may be drawing upon direct questioning, floatback, and affect scan methods to help identify any earlier memories contributing to your new triggers—the ones that are not connected to your initial touchstone memory. It is recommended to start with direct questioning first, then the floatback technique if additional probing is needed, followed by the affect scan.

Let's put this into practice! Bring to mind any recent difficulty you made note of in your TICES log that wasn't connected to the touchstone memory you just completed. Are there any earlier memories that mirror this experience? If you're unable to see any obvious connection there, no worries! Try the following floatback technique:

1. Hold in mind the current disturbing situation.

2. What negative thoughts, emotions, and sensations in your body do you notice having about yourself as you hold it in mind?

3. Notice the image that comes to mind, the negative thoughts you're having about yourself along with any emotions and sensations, and let your mind float back to an earlier time

when you might have felt this way before and just notice what arises.

You may need to repeat this sequence above to continue working your way to earlier and earlier memories. Ideally, this inquiry is able to get you to memories from early to middle childhood. However, if the earliest memory you can identify is from adolescence, or you're having general difficulty putting words to negative thoughts or feelings, try the affect scan method:

1. Hold the experience (either the earliest memory you got to from above, or the current disturbing situation if you did not make earlier connections) in mind.

2. Notice the emotions you're having right now and what you're feeling in your body. Remember to observe these experiences without judgment so you can gently stay with them. You're doing great!

3. Now, holding this experience all together in stillness, let your mind scan back to an earlier time when you might have felt this way before and just notice what comes up.

You may actually notice during this process that the present triggers will continue to inform what past memories are still "dysfunctionally stored" and need to be targeted in the future. Hopefully, you can see this as a flowing process in which your subconscious helps to intuitively inform what memory you will want to target next. Remember that most people with depression driven by childhood trauma will typically go through a full EMDR therapy protocol with about ten disturbing childhood memories in order to comprehensively address the wounds of the past that will empower them to fully engage in their present life. You will complete standard procedures for phases 3–6 for the next touchstone memory you target, closing and opening a session with procedures for phases 7 and 8. Then once you complete *that* touchstone memory, you will return to the present-day triggers connected to those to make sure they're clear, and complete phases 3–6 for any that aren't. *You'll keep repeating this cycle for each new touchstone memory you target.*

One important reminder as you're considering what childhood memories to target: it is typically better to approach the reprocessing *chronologically*, starting with the earliest possible memory *first* and then choosing subsequent targets based on chronological age. As mentioned during the initial assessment phase (1), this typically allows for more efficient processing of dysfunctional material as it will maximize the likelihood of neutralizing the present-day situations. Notice that the word "typically" is used here because sometimes your instincts, informed by the new triggers or a need to prioritize a certain presenting issue, might actually nudge you to focus on a particular childhood memory even if there is another one that happened chronologically earlier. Trust your instincts!

Sometimes people prefer to hold off on starting reprocessing for a memory that feels like the hardest or most difficult one, and that's okay. This is often the case for people who have a history of sexual abuse and may prefer to address other targets rather than immediately addressing memories of that abuse at the outset. This makes perfect sense to not address right away until they've gotten more experience and comfort with EMDR and are savvier at regulating painful emotions that surface during the process! It's also okay if you do feel ready to address something extremely painful at the outset. As long as you're identifying and addressing dysfunctional material you are on track toward acceptance and transformation.

Working on the Future: Incorporating a Future Template

Once you have identified and sufficiently reprocessed childhood trauma, and have addressed any present disturbances, congratulate yourself for accomplishing such major milestones in your personal healing journey! The third prong of the EMDR protocol invites you to consider how you will respond in the future. Ideally, your future responses to difficult situations are congruent with your evolved and most authentic expression of yourself. As mentioned before, treatment is not considered complete until there is a clear integration of yourself in a healthy social system, which is measured by an alternative behavioral response pattern that EMDR refers to as representing a *future template*. Depending on your unique situation and personal history, this could look like being more assertive, expressive, or vulnerable with others, having either less rigid or more rigid boundaries in relationships, being open to a romantic relationship again, leaving unhealthy or incompatible environments, pursuing aligned and meaningful short- and long-term goals, or eliminating reliance on addictive behaviors to name a few. Reference your notes from during the assessment phase (1) covered in chapter 4, where you identified future desired responses. Do these still align with where you are now?

If you have come this far, the chances are high that you are *already* responding differently in the systems in which you operate, whether that be work, home, family of origin, social, or other relevant communities. With the ongoing self-reflections in between sessions, hopefully you have been able to recognize both the internal and external changes you're making and are celebrating them joyfully. Hopefully you are bringing any anxieties and fears you're having about these changes to therapy for any needed additional support. Perhaps there are certain people or situations where you need additional support in responding in ways that are congruent with your newly developed positive cognitions of yourself as worthy, lovable, adequate, and strong.

The third prong of the EMDR therapy protocol uses techniques similar to the resource development and installation exercise you completed during phase 2; these are to help empower you to continue responding in authentic ways in your future. This prong is an incredibly crucial part of treatment as it propels you into continued positive action to create the life you truly desire and deserve. The incorporation of a positive template for relevant future action is essentially an expansion upon the installation phase (5). Research shows that imagining positive outcomes with visualization techniques such as those EMDR uses assists with the learning process and thereby increases chances for success— almost like manifesting your dreams!

Just as the positive cognition is installed after a target memory is sufficiently processed, the incorporation of a future template should not be attempted until both the relevant past and present disturbances are fully processed. As such, you are likely saving this essential exercise until the very end—consider it the cherry on top! Since new and more adaptive positive cognitions are more readily accessible after dysfunctional material is processed, you can also envision more adaptive actions from this state, which you can enhance using bilateral stimulation before you put these into practice in your real life. This exercise includes four general parts, each of which involve multiple steps:

1. Identify your desired outcome

2. Imagine the future scene

3. Run a movie

4. Generate a challenge situation

To start this exercise, you have likely just completed work on either a present trigger or a touchstone memory in which the present trigger was rooted. Either way, you concluded this work with a positive cognition that you enhanced with bilateral stimulation. Bring up this positive belief again. Can you imagine a time in the future when this positive cognition might be useful in the same type of situation you just worked on? Complete the following steps:

1. Identify a future situation, similar to the reprocessed present trigger, where a more adaptive response is needed. *What is the future situation?* Write this situation down once you have it.

2. *Do the words of your positive cognition still fit?* If not, identify a more fitting positive belief and write it down.

3. *How would you like to feel in that future situation?* Write down the desired feeling or state for this future situation.

4. *Imagine yourself responding effectively in that situation in the future.* With your new positive cognition and your desired feeling, imagine stepping into this scene. Take a few moments in silence to notice how you are handling the situation and what you are thinking, feeling, and

experiencing in your body. *What are you noticing?* Write down your experience.

If your response is positive, reinforce the scene and strengthen it with one or two cycles (twenty to forty sets each) of fast bilateral stimulation. Then, bring up the future situation and your positive belief. *On a scale from 1–7, with 1 being completely false and 7 being completely true, how true do they feel to you now?* Record your VOC. Then, *hold the situation and your positive belief together* as you start fast bilateral stimulation (twenty to forty sets). *Take a breath, let it go. What are you noticing now?* Note your response, and then *go with that* as you continue fast bilateral stimulation for twenty to forty sets. Continue this sequence as long as the material is related to the future situation and is becoming more positive or adaptive, or residual disturbance is being processed. Recheck the VOC when it seems appropriate to do so, and add sets of fast bilateral stimulation until the VOC no longer strengthens. Once the VOC reaches a 7, add another set of fast bilateral stimulation, notice and record your experience, and then proceed directly to step 5 below.

If your response is negative or uncertain, explore and address as needed:

1. Is the disturbance because of unfamiliarity or needed skills? Anxiety is normal when you're doing something new! You may just need to start with step 4 again.

2. Sometimes any blocks, anxieties, or fears can be directly reprocessed by doing sets of fast bilateral stimulation until they resolve themselves naturally. So keep going and see where it leads, returning to the beginning of the procedure if need be.

3. If the disturbance is still not clearing, consider whether there are any other present triggers that need to be reprocessed, then proceed to reprocess them using standard procedures for phases 3–6. Then return to the beginning of this step (4).

4. If after the above steps, the future template remains blocked, explore the possibility of potential feeder

memories or associated blocking beliefs. Once those are identified, apply phases 3–6 to reprocess any associated past memories connected to a negative or blocking belief. Then try to come back to this step (4) starting from the beginning.

5. Now, run a movie through your head of dealing effectively with this situation, holding in mind your positive belief about yourself and noticing the positive feelings and sensations. You'll do this step *without* bilateral stimulation first. When you've completed this, *what are you noticing?*

   If your response is positive, *run the movie again* while you complete a set of fast bilateral stimulation. This is to strengthen the positive feelings you're associating with this experience. Then repeat the same procedures from step 4 to link the desired positive cognition with the future template. Once the VOC is a 7 add another set of fast bilateral stimulation, notice and record your experience, and then proceed directly to step 6 below.

   If you come across any blocks, continue to run the movie in your head repeatedly from start to finish, pausing to process the experience in between. This repeated exposure will help to naturally reduce anxiety and increase your confidence. Then you can apply sets of fast bilateral stimulation as in the procedure above when the response is neutral or positive.

6. Imagine that same situation, but this time a challenge occurs. *What would the challenge be?* Write down this possible challenge.

7. Adopt the attitude of *challenge accepted!* Go ahead and implement steps 4 and 5 above for this situation with the added challenge. You may choose to generate multiple challenge situations if it seems appropriate or if time allows.

8. Use standard procedures for the closure phase (7) at the end of every session.

Summary

Hopefully, you've come away from this chapter with a better sense of the ongoing reevaluation phase throughout EMDR therapy once you've started the reprocessing phases, and how to ensure your inner work is fully integrated across the three-pronged protocol. Typically speaking, the future template is saved for the very end of treatment as you're prioritizing addressing the adverse childhood memories contributing to present-day triggers of depression first. Otherwise, if you try developing a future template too soon, it will likely take you back to past memories that would block the template's ability to be fully positive. The following outline briefly summarizes what you learned in this chapter and can be used as a helpful guide with regard to treatment plan considerations.

1. Evaluate whether the touchstone memory is resolved (SUD = 0, VOC > 6, clear body scan) and, where needed, continue reprocessing phases to work toward resolution.

2. Check remaining experiences identified during phase 1, as well as associations that emerged during reprocessing sessions:

Past

- Reprocess other touchstone memories that are still disturbing.

- Apply standard procedures for phases 3–6 until sufficiently processed.

Present

- Reprocess present triggers that are still disturbing.

- Apply standard procedures for phases 3–6 for each trigger that did not neutralize from reprocessing past experiences.

Future Templates

- After a present trigger is reprocessed, proceed to procedural steps for incorporating a future template.

CHAPTER 9

Conclusion: Maintaining and Spreading Your Rekindled Love

Be the change that you wish to see in the world.

—Mahatma Gandhi

Going inward to face and heal the roots of your depression is an act of self-compassion, but it is also an act of service to the world at large. Think about it this way: when you commit to your own self-love and self-acceptance, this in turn influences your surrounding communities, heals generational wounds, and stops them from being passed down, therefore bettering future generations: a *ripple effect*. Therefore, the energy you've spent, the time you've invested, and the courage you've shown are some of the most selfless, profound work you can do.

In other words, *you are making a big difference!* Your increasingly healed and renewed energy influences and inspires others in the most meaningful ways. Learning to fulfill your own unmet needs by becoming a nurturing, protective caregiver to yourself is not only personally meaningful, but it makes you a more compassionate and aligned person. Imagine if the world as a whole were more self-compassionate and living in alignment—that kind of energy would make a momentous impact on the evolution of the planet.

In this way, the work continues. Self-love is not a destination so much as it is an ongoing journey and overall lifestyle. It's about how you treat and show up for yourself every day. How has this journey brought you closer to the home within yourself you've been longing for?

During the first phase of EMDR, you were advised to keep an ongoing list of positive experiences of yourself. What have you added to this list and what can you add right now when you look back at memories of yourself at work during your EMDR sessions? Find ways to genuinely appreciate what each and every aspect of the journey has offered you for your evolution, healing, and growth—especially those most difficult moments for which we often have the hardest time expressing gratitude. All of it has been worth it! Allow yourself some moments in silence to savor these feelings of appreciation and gratitude. You deserve it.

Maintenance Plan: A Lifestyle of Self-Love

Imagine buying a very vulnerable plant—one that requires regular care and maintenance. Then imagine not giving it the proper amount of sunlight, water, or soil. What's going to happen? For one, the plant is not going to grow much. It will fight hard to survive, but soon it will start to wilt away and take much extra work to try and revive; eventually, it may completely die off if it is entirely neglected. Alternatively, when the plant is properly taken care of, it grows beautifully, strengthening its underground roots, which allows it to not only continue to grow but to also thrive!

In the context of the proper maintenance of your alleviated depression symptoms, it may be helpful to consider this analogy to remember that you, too, are a vulnerable plant who needs sufficient tenderness, love, and care from your roots all the way to your highest branches, stems, or leaves. Seriously implement the words *take care* so you can be a thriving plant to benefit both yourself and the world around you. As a thriving plant, how are you fulfilling your own needs for sunlight, soil, and water? As always, in service of self-love, take a few moments in your journal to jot down your thoughts about this question before reading ahead. You might also pull up your list of internal and external resources from chapter 4 to add to, edit, and revise.

Basic Needs

First and foremost, make sure you are prioritizing your *basic needs*. This includes food, water, rest, sleep, sunlight, and physical activity. The benefits of meeting your basic needs cannot be undervalued, as your investment in your health will give you the greatest returns in the short and long term. Eat nourishing meals that primarily consist of whole, plant-based foods and generally make your heart happy, but don't hold back from indulging in your inner child's favorite treats in moderation, too. Keep yourself hydrated—more so on the days when you're especially active or otherwise shedding more tears. Practice connecting with, listening to, and trusting your body's cues.

Sleep quality is absolutely paramount to physical, cognitive, emotional, and mental health; it can even help to prevent depression and suicidal thoughts. As such, aim for about 7–9 hours of sleep every night in addition to listening to your needs for additional rest. The following are some important practices to implement in order to maximize your sleep quality:

- Wake up and get out of bed at roughly the same day *every day*—even on non-work days. Aim to expose yourself to natural sunlight. If possible, do this *as soon as you wake up*— this will help set your circadian clock, thereby regulating your sleep-wake cycle and improving your energy.

- Only use your bed for sleeping or sexual activity—doing anything else in bed may unintentionally cause your mind to associate the bed with being alert and awake, which is counterproductive for sleep.

- Only go to bed when you are sleepy, as sleep cannot be forced.

- If you wake up in the middle of the night and cannot get back to sleep, get out of bed and engage in something relatively mundane and screen-free, such as folding laundry, sorting mail, or putting away dishes, until you feel sleepy again. Many people with depression tend to spend too much time in bed so this is especially important.

- Create a *buffer zone* in the 30–60 minutes leading up to your bedtime where your only goal is to relax to help you wind down for sleep. This can include your existing nighttime routine like dental hygiene and skincare routines, and may also include relaxation exercises like those introduced during the preparation phase (2) of EMDR covered in chapter 5.

- Avoid excessive napping during the day as it can interfere with sleeping soundly at night. Brief power naps (about 20–30 minutes) between 7–9 hours after your wake-up time can be beneficial for mental health and productivity.

- Limit use of electronics and make use of the blue light filter on electronic devices when it gets dark outside. The blue light emitted from electronic devices can interfere with your brain's natural release of melatonin, which promotes sleepiness, due to tricking it into thinking it's still light outside.

- Turn your phone over and cover your clocks at night so you don't look at them in the middle of the night if you wake up. Checking the time stimulates your brain which is counterproductive for sleep.

- Pay attention to your caffeine and alcohol intake, as well as eating heavy meals near bedtime. What we put in our bodies affects our sleep and alertness, and can impact our ability to get restful, deep sleep. If you struggle with knowing what this looks like, finding a dietitian can be helpful for guidance that is tailored to your specific needs.

- Exercise is beneficial for mood, energy, and sleep quality, with research demonstrating sleep quality is maximized for those who exercise in the morning (Buman et al. 2013). While it's generally okay to exercise at a time that works best with your style and schedule, use discretion when engaging in higher-intensity exercise less than two hours before bedtime. The concerns here are that it might be too stimulating for your body by increasing your heart rate and body temperature, which can negatively interfere with your sleep-wake cycle; listen to and trust your own experiences here. The US Centers for Disease Control and Prevention (2023) recommend at least 150 minutes of moderate-intensity physical activity a week, or seventy-five minutes of vigorous-intensity, plus at least two days of muscle-strengthening activity each week.

Love and Belonging

Second, make sure you are prioritizing your *love and belonging* needs. If this journey has taught you anything, it's that love is what makes us grow and thrive. Love is the most meaningful thing. So let love in! Cherish the beings in your life who you trust genuinely care for you, and vice versa, and continue to nourish these connections in the same way that you're better nourishing yourself. The connections that lift your spirit while at the same time challenge and inspire you are the most meaningful.

Aim to continue to build and maintain a loving and supportive community around you. Spend quality time with your people, and balance giving and receiving support. This might look like sharing uplifting or funny videos, photos, or memes regularly to show that you're thinking of and staying connected with them. Doing these simple things also helps you bring more joy and laughter to your life, which can have an impactful ripple effect. Other ways to maintain a connection to those around you include providing a listening ear, engaging in activities together, snuggling, hugging, sharing a hobby, or watching a movie together. Learn to savor and cherish these moments of connection. No matter how introverted or independent you are, the truth is we are social animals and we not only need one another but thrive on learning from and teaching each other. Remember that, as someone who feels worthy of love and being appropriately cared for, it's okay to have needs and to respectfully and patiently ask for extra support during times when you may need it most. You deserve it just as much as anyone else.

Many people find that as they evolve and grow, certain people, settings, and environments may no longer be in alignment with their highest truths. As such, you may have to officially snip away certain stems, leaves, and branches. Trust in your resilience. Trust that new connections and spaces will enter your life as you continue to take care of yourself. Sometimes the most compassionate thing you can do for both yourself and another is set a boundary, let go with grace, and trust in yourself—appreciate the lessons learned and the courage you've tapped into, continuing to nourish yourself.

Spiritual Connectedness

Third, engage in ongoing practices that are nourishing for your spirit. This can look like religious practices or rituals, but it doesn't have to be. The purpose of such practices is to promote feelings of connectedness, peace, release, and joy. For some, these practices might include going on a nature walk or otherwise spending time outdoors, engaging your senses, and grounding you in the present moment. Some other ideas include:

- Meditation

- Yoga

- Coloring books

- Knitting

- Creating writing or journaling

- Reading

- Playing a sport

- Listening to music

- Playing an instrument

- Singing

- Dancing

- Brewing and sipping your favorite hot beverage

Compassionate Self-Reflection

Remember that mindfulness and self-compassion are skills that do not come naturally and must therefore be practiced consistently and regularly. Consider practicing an extension of the reevaluation phase (8) by engaging in self-reflections and daily journaling where you check in with yourself. If your ingrained pattern has been to suppress or avoid your emotions, maintaining the reversal of this habit is going to require continuous practice. It is normal to compartmentalize your feelings while you are functioning at work or school, *and* it is important that you take the time and space to decompartmentalize and process feelings to keep strengthening these newer ways of relating to yourself.

Journaling is a particularly helpful outlet to continue practicing mindful self-awareness and self-compassion. There are endless ways to approach journaling; follow your inner voice with regard to how you do this. You may find that some entries are longer than others, or that you have more time over the weekends and at the outset of the week rather than in the middle of the week. This is okay, as it is better to spend even just a few minutes a day rather than none at all. Try your best and appreciate your efforts so they can be properly reinforced. In service of continuing the practice of decompartmentalizing your emotions using mindfulness and self-compassion, the following are some suggestions for these brief check-ins:

- Imagine being a caring, compassionate, and curious parent, friend, mentor, or coach to yourself for each entry you make—again, practice being that loving, caring person to yourself that you wish to experience from others.

- Don't hesitate to truly turn inward, asking questions and engaging in conversation and open reflections.

- Some probing questions like a simple *how are you feeling right now?* or *how was your day today?* are a good starting place.

- Consider reviewing a "rose" and a "thorn" of the day. That is, *what were some successes from today that you can draw out and appreciate about yourself? What were some challenges you came across? What can you appreciate and learn from these challenges moving forward?*

- This brief check-in can help you decompartmentalize any emotions, and therefore give you a space to practice mindful awareness of them as you're journaling. You can integrate mindful awareness and self-compassion by writing out a description of what you're feeling in the here and now in your body and mind without judgment, and then you can allow yourself some time in stillness to be lovingly present with those feelings so they can be truly felt. You can then go back to your journal to process what this experience was like and offer yourself positive affirmations and words of encouragement to reinforce this practice. Each time you do this, you are cultivating acceptance of your experience and strengthening self-love.

- Use the information communicated from your check-in to consider your schedule and intentions for the day ahead. What might need to be adjusted or tweaked based on this information? It can be helpful to outline your schedule for the next day (or even the week ahead), and to set your intentions for how you wish to feel as you conquer the future.

- If you foresee any challenges, this is a great opportunity to integrate a future template from the reevaluation or preparation phases of EMDR, respectively. It may be helpful to continue integrating positive affirmations and words of encouragement, too, especially in the closing of each of your entries.

- If the challenges that arise come from deeper layers of adverse childhood experiences or repressed experiences coming to the light, trust that this is often a part of how the journey works and not at all an indication that you're going backward; quite the opposite. Grief does not happen all at once and is a journey in and of itself. Each time you notice grief arising is an opportunity to practice mindful awareness and self-compassion. Consider eliciting additional therapy support if repressed experiences emerge, and appreciate your continued evolution and growth evident in the surfacing of deeper layers.

Gratitude

Notice in the above suggestions that an emphasis is made on not only considering your day but also reflecting upon what you can *appreciate* about the full range of roses and thorns from the day. The intention here is to train your brain to embody an attitude of *gratitude* whether the experience is pleasant or not. Take the time to not only draw out at least three moments or experiences from each day that you feel grateful for, but to savor the feelings that arise during the exercise itself. This ongoing practice will help rewire your brain to feel more appreciation and joy— especially when you can express thankfulness for the unpleasant experiences—which over time can help you consistently feel and let in more happiness. After all, happiness is about appreciating what you have *now*. Gratitude practice is therefore a direct pathway to happiness because you are deliberately cultivating an appreciation of your day-to-day experiences.

Generosity

Last but certainly not least, *be of service to others by living true to your heart and being unapologetically you*. Give generously from your heart and with the purest of intentions. You and those around you will benefit significantly when you express your love, light, and wisdom—especially now that you've found and owned your truth. Take a moment to

congratulate yourself for engaging in this deep inner work! Return back
to your motivations and *why* from the values exploration and clarification exercises covered in the last section of chapter 3. Remember the
future world you envision and how you intend to show up in this world
across your various roles. Trust and believe in yourself unconditionally,
and stay committed to your truth.

Your EMDR for Depression Journey

Don't be pushed around by the fears in your mind. Be led by the dreams in your heart.

–Roy T. Bennett

In this book, you have learned about depression as not only a personal but a universal public health problem that is often rooted in unprocessed childhood trauma of varying sorts—especially those involving emotional neglect and abuse. You have come to understand the many ways that depression can manifest and that, despite how it manifests, the main goal of a comprehensive treatment for depression is to achieve *acceptance*. You have experienced and likely will continue to experience the reality that acceptance is a challenging yet incredibly meaningful journey for healing depression and promoting personal growth. Accompanying this journey are many inevitable twists and turns, each of which helps you develop greater self-awareness, slowly bringing the unconscious processes out of the darkness so that you can rise into and fully align with all that you truly are.

This book has given you essential education and tools to best pilot this journey. You've learned the importance of and started to apply building the skill of being nonjudgmentally present with your experiences to exercise mindfulness. You've learned how to treat yourself like a best friend and a nurturing and protective parent to develop self-compassion. And you've engaged in exercises to help you identify your truest and purest motivations for doing this work in the first place. Last but not least, you've learned and applied each of the eight phases of EMDR therapy, the separate but connected journeys of which are summarized below to remind you of how much deep inner work you have comprehensively covered.

Phase 1: History Taking and Treatment Planning

During the first phase of EMDR, you identified primary presenting issues that speak to how your depression currently manifests (e.g., low self-esteem, anger or irritability, rumination, worry, anxiety, perfectionism, feelings of inadequacy, self-doubt, etc.). You then identified recent experiences that represent these presenting issues, and learned techniques including direct questioning, floatback, and affect scan to identify root memories being triggered in present-day experiences. This led to developing a list of touchstone memories to target during the EMDR therapy process, an understanding of what memory to start reprocessing, and uncovering other potentially relevant present-day triggers or important contextual factors. Future desired responses to your present triggers were reviewed to identify general goals. Finally, you explored and identified current personal and external resources through a series of questions, as well as further needed resources to increase your resilience and readiness for the reprocessing phases.

Phase 2: Preparation

During the second phase of EMDR, you became equipped with all of the necessary basic education, tools, and understanding to effectively engage in the EMDR process by 1) learning the various forms of bilateral stimulation to use for the reprocessing phases, 2) understanding how EMDR therapy works, 3) recognizing how to apply the dual attention of both past and present when bringing up target memories for reprocessing, and 4) building additional internal resources to help with safety, stabilization, and general emotional regulation during the process. You learned and engaged in multiple exercises to build further internal strength—safe/calm state, container, resource development and installation, relaxation, and grounding exercises—in addition to being encouraged to continue practicing mindfulness and self-compassion exercises daily.

Phase 3: Target Assessment

During the third phase of EMDR, you learned and engaged in the procedures involved in helping you access the memory network that contained the touchstone memory you were targeting for reprocessing at the time. The sequence of sections you covered in this target assessment included 1) labeling the target memory, 2) being given instructions for reprocessing, 3) identifying the worst image or part, 4) identifying the negative cognition, 5) identifying a desired positive cognition to associate with the image and the initial validity of this cognition, 6) identifying emotions associated with the image and negative cognition, 7) identifying your current subjective units of disturbance (SUD) associated with the memory and noting the location of body sensations associated with the disturbance.

Phase 4: Desensitization

You learned that the core of EMDR processing happens during the fourth phase, and that this phase of treatment is typically the longest in duration because of its focus on reprocessing the dysfunctional material until it is no longer disturbing across cognitive, emotional, and physical realms. During this phase, you focused on the target memory and associated negative cognition, emotions, and physical sensations, and simultaneously engaged in sets of fast bilateral stimulation. You practiced trusting your brain's natural ability to heal itself in the manner that it needed to by observing your experience without judgment and making note of the changes you noticed from set to set in the form of thoughts, images, memories, emotions, or sensations. You practiced letting go of control of the process and allowing whatever needed to happen to unfold at its own pace. This phase without a doubt challenged your emotion regulation abilities, expanded your window of tolerance, and strengthened your resilience and self-compassion. During the process, you discovered and tended to the unmet needs of the younger versions of you that feed into your most recent experiences of depression, and you learned how to begin to fulfill those needs by practicing being a more nurturing and protective caregiver to yourself. You continued to engage in this process over multiple sessions as necessary until it felt neutral as indicated by your SUD level going down to 0.

Phase 5: Installation

Once the disturbance associated with each of your touchstone memories went away, you proceeded to the fifth phase of EMDR, during which you focused on strengthening a more adaptive, positive belief to associate with each of the memories. You learned that healing is not only about reducing the distress associated with the past but that it is equally about being able to look back at each touchstone memory you were targeting at the time with clarity, peace, self-efficacy, and self-compassion. The fifth phase then helped you install this more self-loving positive cognition to override the previously held negative cognition and strengthen positive feelings.

Phase 6: Body Scan

To ensure that each of your touchstone memories was sufficiently processed, once completing the installation phase you were guided through a body scan. This sixth phase of EMDR involved focusing on the memory and positive cognition while closing your eyes and scanning your body from head to toe for any sign of residual physical disturbance. Any residual disturbance you identified was then targeted using sets of fast bilateral stimulation for reprocessing and releasing. You learned the importance of ensuring that each memory is fully processed on cognitive, emotional, and physical or somatic levels.

Phase 7: Closure

During the seventh phase of EMDR, you learned how to appropriately close up and transition out of an EMDR therapy session, remembering to first draw upon internal resources you developed during the second phase of treatment as needed to contain disturbing material and come back to a calm state of mind. After confirming a place of safety and stabilization, you gathered your thoughts to make a positive statement summarizing what you learned or gained from the session. You were informed and encouraged to manage expectations in between sessions. Relatedly, you learned about the importance of developing a journal like the TICES log to record any in-between session disturbances, recognizing that the processing can continue after the session, and is important to make note of as it informs your treatment plan and possible next targets in your EMDR therapy process. You were equally encouraged to notice and record any positive triggering experiences in between sessions as well.

Phase 8: Reevaluation

Finally, during the reevaluation phase of treatment, you learned how to begin an EMDR therapy session after starting the reprocessing of a touchstone memory. You learned the importance of reflecting upon how your symptoms, thoughts, feelings, and behaviors have changed since the last session, and what old and new triggers arose in between your sessions. You came to understand that this ongoing reassessment is to ascertain whether the touchstone memory being targeted has been resolved, whether associated material has been triggered that needs to be processed, whether all touchstone memories have been identified and reprocessed, and whether you have fully integrated your more-healed and more-evolved self within your social networks. You learned about the standard three-pronged protocol of EMDR therapy, recognizing that once the past experiences and present triggers are sufficiently processed, it is important to empower yourself for the future. In closing, you then learned and engaged in a positive future template exercise to expand upon and strengthen the positive cognitions you've recently installed.

What an incredible feat to have comprehensively covered confronting and working through your psyche! Take a moment to think about where you were mentally, emotionally, psychologically, and spiritually before you started this journey so you can recognize and appreciate each of the ways in which you have evolved and grown up to this point. Think about the limiting beliefs about yourself that you have uncovered and overridden with many hours of reprocessing, reflecting, and reprogramming yourself in service of your fullest alignment. Continue to add to your ever-growing list of positive experiences of yourself, and keep showing up for yourself in the ways that you deserve every single day!

Acknowledgments

First of all, thank you to New Harbinger Publications for finding me and believing in me to help make this meaningful contribution as I continue striving toward my mission. I hadn't imagined I'd be writing my first book until much later in life. I especially hadn't imagined how deeply healing the challenges of creating this comprehensive book would be. It's been an adventurous journey of its own and Little Lara is overflowing with joy.

Speaking of Little Lara, this book would literally not be possible without her as well as my future children, grandchildren, and generations to follow—my love for you has been my personal *why*. And Daylen and Sienna. And Soco who's furrever modeling being unapologetically expressive, probably thanks to the imprints left by our beloved Momo. All of you truly are magical little beings.

To Grandma, Mom, and Jana—the strong, witty women in my immediate lineage whom I was blessed to grow up beside and who, along with Carolyn, modeled eloquence with words. To Chad and Tyler, the big brothers who gave the gifts of joy and goofiness. To Grandpa, who inspired me the most in terms of excelling in education and the arts with a discerning eye. And to Jerry, who believed in my character and provided for my education.

To my beautiful community of friends both near and far who have helped ground me while at the same time lifting me up through extending compassion, loving me unconditionally, and supporting my wild side.

To my past, present, and future clients, students, supervisees, and consultees for trusting me, triggering my own deeper layers of stuff, and giving me the gifts of ever-growing wisdom, competence, and confidence.

To Francine Shapiro for discovering and founding EMDR which, alongside mindfulness, self-compassion, and journaling, has been an integral component in my own healing journey.

And to Nick, for just about everything. You know I don't like to judge, but I think you're my favorite. You've loved, challenged, and trusted in me like no one ever has, and you are the Yoda master of strength, courage, and independence. I truly am deeply grateful you exist. I love you and always will.

References

Adshead, G., and S. Ferris. 2007. "Treatment of Victims of Trauma." *Advances in Psychiatric Treatment* 13 (5): 358–368.

Agid, O., B. Shapira, J. Zislin, M. Ritsner, B. Hanin, H. Murad, T. Troudart, M. Bloch, U. Heresco-Levy, and B. Lerer. 1999. "Environment and Vulnerability to Major Psychiatric Illness: A Case Control Study of Early Parental Loss in Major Depression, Bipolar Disorder and Schizophrenia." *Molecular Psychiatry* 4 (2): 163–172.

Bleich, A., M. Koslowsky, A. Dolev, and B. Lerer. 1997. "Post-traumatic Stress Disorder and Depression: An Analysis of Comorbidity." *The British Journal of Psychiatry* 170 (5): 479–482.

Boterhoven de Haan, K. L., C. W. Lee, E. Fassbinder, S. M. van Es, S. Menninga, M. Meewisse, M. Rijkeboer, M. Kousemaker, and A. Arntz. 2020. "Imagery Rescripting and Eye Movement Desensitisation and Reprocessing as Treatment for Adults with Post-traumatic Stress disorder from Childhood Trauma: Randomised Clinical Trial." *The British Journal of Psychiatry* 217 (5): 609–615.

Buman, M. P., B. A. Phillips, S. D. Youngstedt, C. E. Kline, and M. Hirshkowitz. 2014. "Does Nighttime Exercise Really Disturb Sleep? Results from the 2013 National Sleep Foundation Sleep in America Poll." *Sleep Medicine* 15 (7): 755–761.

Chapman, D. P., C. L. Whitfield, V. J. Felitti, S. R. Dube, V. J. Edwards, and R. F. Anda. 2004. "Adverse Childhood Experiences and the Risk of Depressive Disorders in Adulthood." *Journal of Affective Disorders* 82 (2): 217–225.

De Jongh, A., C. de Roos, and S. El-Leithy. 2024. "State of the Science: Eye Movement Desensitization and Reprocessing (EMDR) Therapy." *Journal of Traumatic Stress* 37 (2): 205–216.

Edwards, V. J., G. W. Holden, V. J. Felitti, and R. F. Anda. 2003. "Relationship Between Multiple Forms of Childhood Maltreatment and Adult Mental Health in Community Respondents: Results from the Adverse Childhood Experiences Study." *American Journal of Psychiatry* 160 (8): 1453–1460.

Felitti, V. J., R. F. Anda, D. Nordenberg, D. E. Williamson, A. M. Spitz, V. Edwards, J. S. Marks. 1998. "Relationship of Childhood Abuse and Household Dysfunction to Many of the Leading Causes of Death in Adults. The Adverse Childhood Experiences (ACE) Study." *American Journal of Preventive Medicine* 14: 245–58.

Goodwin, R. D., L. C. Dierker, M. Wu, S. Galea, C. W. Hoven, and A. H. Weinberger, A. H. 2022. "Trends in U.S. Depression Prevalence from 2015 to 2020: The Widening Treatment Gap." *American Journal of Preventive Medicine* 63 (5): 726–733.

Griffioen, B. T., A. A. van der Vegt, I. W. de Groot, and A. de Jongh. 2017. "The Effect of EMDR and CBT on Low Self-Esteem in a General Psychiatric Population: A Randomized Controlled Trial." *Frontiers in Psychology* 8: 1910.

Hase, M., J. Plagge, A. Hase, R. Braas, L. Ostacoli, A. Hofmann, and C. Huchzermeier. 2018. "Eye Movement Desensitization and Reprocessing Versus Treatment as Usual in the Treatment of Depression: A Randomized-Controlled Trial." *Frontiers in Psychology* 9 (1384): 1–12.

Hofmann, A., A. Hilgers, M. Lehnung, P. Liebermann, L. Ostacoli, W. Schneider, and M. Hase. 2014. "Eye Movement Desensitization and Reprocessing as an Adjunctive Treatment of Unipolar Depression: A Controlled Study." *Journal of EMDR Practice and Research* 8 (3): 103–112.

Kabat-Zinn, J. "Mindfulness-Based Interventions in Context: Past, Present and Future." 2003. *Clinical Psychology: Science and Practice* 10 (2): 144–156.

Kendler, K. S., R. C. Kessler, M. C. Neale, A. C. Heath, and L. J. Eaves. 1993. "The Prediction of Major Depression in Women: Toward an Integrated Etiologic Model." *American Journal of Psychiatry* 150 (8): 1139–1148.

Kendler, K. S., C. M. Bulik, J. Silberg, J. M. Hettema, J. Myers, and C. A. Prescott. 2000. "Childhood Sexual Abuse and Adult Psychiatric and Substance Use Disorders in Women: An Epidemiological and Cotwin Control Analysis." *Archives of General Psychiatry* 57 (10): 953–959.

Magnus. J., A. Shankar, and D. Broussard. 2010. "Self-Report of Depressive Symptoms in African American and White Women in Primary Care." *Journal of the National Medical Association* 102 (5): 389–395.

Mandelli, L., C. Petrelli, and A. Serretti. 2015. "The Role of Specific Early Trauma in Adult Depression: A Meta-Analysis of Published Literature. Childhood trauma and Adult Depression." *European Psychiatry* 30 (6): 665–680.

Matthijssen, S. J., T. C. Brouwers, and A. de Jongh. 2024. "Visual Schema Displacement Therapy Versus Eye Movement Desensitization and Reprocessing Therapy Versus Waitlist in the Treatment of Post-traumatic Stress Disorder: Results of a Randomized Clinical Trial." *Frontiers in Psychiatry* 15.

Neff, K.D. 2003. "Self-Compassion: An Alternative Conceptualization of a Healthy Attitude Toward Oneself." *Self and Identity* 2 (2): 85–102.

Negele, A., J. Kaufhold, L. Kallenbach, and M. Leuzinger-Bohleber, M. 2015. "Childhood Trauma and Its Relation to Chronic Depression in Adulthood." *Depression Research and Treatment* 2015 (1).

Nelson, E. C., A. C. Heath, P. A. Madden, M. L. Cooper, S. H. Dinwiddie, K. K. Bucholz, A. Glowinski, T. McLaughlin, M. P. Dunne, D. J. Statham, and N. G. Martin. 2002. "Association Between Self-Reported Childhood Sexual Abuse and Adverse Psychosocial Outcomes: Results from a Twin Study." *Archives of General Psychiatry* 59 (2): 139–145.

Ostacoli, L., S. Carletto, M. Cavallo, P. Baldomir-Gago, P., G. di Lorenzo, I. Fernandez, M. Hase, A. Justo-Alonso, M. Lehnung, G. Migliaretti, F. Oliva, M. Pagani, S. Recarey-Eiris, R. Torta, V. Tumani, A. I. Gonzalez-Vazquez, and A. Hofmann. 2018. "Comparison of Eye Movement Desensitization Reprocessing and Cognitive Behavioral Therapy as Adjunctive Treatments for Recurrent Depression: The European Depression EMDR Network (EDEN) Randomized Controlled Trial." *Frontiers in Psychology* 9 (74): 1–12.

Schnurr, P. P., J. L. Hamblen, J. Wolf, R. Coller, C. Collie, M. A. Fuller, P. E. Holtzheimer, U. Kelly, A. J. Lang, K. McGraw, J. C. Morganstein, S. B. Norman, K. Papke, I. Petrakis, D. Riggs, J. A. Sall, B. Shiner, I. Wiechers, and M. S. Kelber. 2024. "The Management of Posttraumatic Stress Disorder and Acute Stress Disorder: Synopsis of the 2023 U.S. Department of Veterans Affairs and U.S. Department of Defense Clinical Practice Guideline." *Annals of Internal Medicine* 177 (3): 363–374.

Seok, J. W., and J. I. Kim. 2024. "The Efficacy of Eye Movement Desensitization and Reprocessing Treatment for Depression: A Meta-Analysis and Meta-Regression of Randomized Controlled Trials." *Journal of Clinical Medicine* 13 (18): 5633.

Shalev, A. Y., S. Freedman, T. Peri, D. Brandes, T. Sahar, S. P. Orr, and R. K. Pitman. 1998. "Prospective Study of Posttraumatic Stress Disorder and Depression Following Trauma." *American Journal of Psychiatry* 155 (5): 630–637.

Shapiro, F. 2017. *Eye Movement Desensitization and Reprocessing (EMDR) Therapy: Basic Principles, Protocols, and Procedures.* Guilford Publications.

U.S. Centers for Disease Control and Prevention. 2023. "Adult Activity: An Overview." Accessed June 1, 2025. https://www.cdc.gov/physical-activity-basics/guidelines/adults.html.

Van der Kolk, B. A., J. Spinazzola, M. E. Blaustein, J. W. Hopper, E. K. Hopper, D. L. Korn, and W. B. Simpson. 2007. "A Randomized Clinical Trial of Eye Movement Desensitization and Reprocessing (EMDR), Fluoxetine, and Pill Placebo in the Treatment of Posttraumatic Stress Disorder: Treatment Effects and Long-Term Maintenance." *Journal of Clinical Psychiatry* 68 (1): 37–46.

Vittengl, J. R., L. A. Clark, T. W. Dunn, and R. B. Jarrett. 2007. "Reducing Relapse and Recurrence in Unipolar Depression: A Comparative Meta-Analysis of Cognitive-Behavioral Therapy's Effects." *Journal of Consulting and Clinical Psychology* 75: 475–488.

Waite, R., and P.A. Shewokis. 2012. "Childhood Trauma and Adult Self-Reported Depression." *Association of Black Nursing Faculty Journal* 23 (1): 8–13.

World Health Organization. 2022. "COVID-19 Pandemic Triggers 25% Increase in Prevalence of Anxiety and Depression Worldwide." Accessed June 1, 2025. https://www.who.int/news/item/02-03-2022-covid-19-pandemic-triggers-25-increase-in-prevalence-of-anxiety-and-depression-worldwide.

World Health Organization. 2023a. "Billions Left Behind on the Path to Universal Health Coverage." Accessed June 1, 2025. https://www.who.int/news/item/18-09-2023-billions-left-behind-on-the-path-to-universal-health-coverage.

World Health Organization. 2023b. "Depressive Disorder (Depression)." Accessed June 1, 2025. https://www.who.int/news-room/fact-sheets/detail/depression.

Yehuda, R., E. Vermetten, and A. McFarlane. 2012. "Understanding Depression as it Occurs in the Context of Post-traumatic Stress Disorder." *Depression Research and Treatment* 2012.

Lara Barbir, PsyD, is a clinical psychologist and founder of Transcendent Therapy in California. She also holds a faculty appointment with The Chicago School of Professional Psychology. Through her clinical work, teaching, speaking, and training, she is on a mission to create a world of more emotionally secure parents and future generations. She is particularly passionate about using eye movement desensitization and reprocessing (EMDR) and interpersonal psychotherapy approaches with higher-functioning adults and teens struggling with depression, complex trauma/post-traumatic stress disorder (PTSD), anxiety, insomnia, and chronic pain. Prior to starting her private practice, she worked in the VA hospital setting for more than six years. She received her doctorate in counseling psychology from Radford University in Virginia.

Real change *is* possible

For more than fifty years, New Harbinger has published proven-effective self-help books and pioneering workbooks to help readers of all ages and backgrounds improve mental health and well-being, and achieve lasting personal growth. In addition, our spirituality books offer profound guidance for deepening awareness and cultivating healing, self-discovery, and fulfillment.

Founded by psychologist Matthew McKay and Patrick Fanning, New Harbinger is proud to be an independent, employee-owned company. Our books reflect our core values of integrity, innovation, commitment, sustainability, compassion, and trust. Written by leaders in the field and recommended by therapists worldwide, New Harbinger books are practical, accessible, and provide real tools for real change.

newharbingerpublications

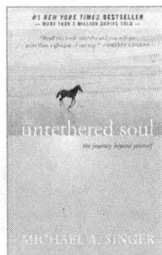

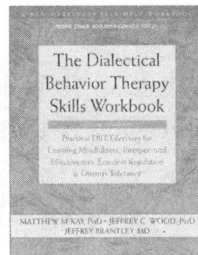

Did you know there are **free tools** you can download for this book?

Free tools are things like **worksheets, guided meditation exercises**, and **more** that will help you get the most out of your book.

You can download free tools for this book—whether you bought or borrowed it, in any format, from any source—from the New Harbinger website. All you need is a NewHarbinger.com account. Just use the URL provided in this book to view the free tools that are available for it. Then, click on the "download" button for the free tool you want, and follow the prompts that appear to log in to your NewHarbinger.com account and download the material.

You can also save the free tools for this book to your **Free Tools Library** so you can access them again anytime, just by logging in to your account! Just look for this button on the book's free tools page.

+ Save this to my free tools library

If you need help accessing or downloading free tools, visit **newharbinger.com/faq** or contact us at **customerservice@newharbinger.com**.

"Lara Barbir shows us, with clarity and depth, the connection between trauma and depression. Thanks to her reassuring style, we find out we are not to blame when we feel bad. We discover that self-acceptance is not an impossible dream but a skill we can *learn*. We see how eye movement desensitization and reprocessing (EMDR) takes all that we are and have experienced and makes it unconditionally workable. Then trauma is not a dead end, but a door."

—**David Richo, PhD**, author of *Triggers*

"In this compassionate and practical book, Lara Barbir offers a clear path for understanding and healing depression rooted in trauma. With warmth and clinical wisdom, she shows how EMDR therapy can transform pain into resilience. A vital resource for both clients and clinicians."

—**Arielle Schwartz, PhD**, coauthor of *EMDR Therapy and Somatic Psychology*

"Lara Barbir has created an exceptional, comprehensive guide to EMDR for depression. She brings such warmth and clarity to this complex topic. The book is a thorough, well-structured, and engaging read. It seamlessly blends research and practical strategies for easy-to-understand application. It's both an invaluable reference for therapists and an approachable, enlightening read for the public."

—**Erin Madden, LCSW, ICADC, CAP**, certified EMDR therapist and EMDRIA-Approved Consultant